Wicked MISSISSIPPI

Wicked MISSISSIPPI

RYAN STARRETT AND JOSH FOREMAN
Foreword by Sarah Fowler

THE
History
PRESS

Published by The History Press
Charleston, SC
www.historypress.com

First published 2024

Manufactured in the United States

ISBN 9781467157599

Library of Congress Control Number: 2024935388

To the journalists of Bruin News Now *who, after informing and entertaining their classmates and teachers at Saint Joseph Catholic School, took their talents to the next level. Special thanks to John Baladi and Emma Dotson (MSU), Hannah Dear (Ole Miss), Garret Grove (USM) and Gia Picarella (LSU). Your talents are indisputable, and your characters are just what this world needs.* Ita inflammate omnia*!*

To Joseph and Penelope (again).
Don't be like the people in this book—especially that guy in chapter twelve.
Be better!

—RYAN STARRETT

....

To Georgia Hamilton, Dylan Bufkin, Hannah Blankenship, Heather Harrison, Joshua Britt and the many other editors who have worked to make the Reflector—*the student voice of Mississippi State University since 1884— excellent for the last five years. I appreciate you.*

—JOSH FOREMAN

CONTENTS

SLOTH

GREED

GLUTTONY

LUST

FOREWORD

*E*very day, church bells ring out through downtown Jackson. I worked in downtown Jackson for nearly seven years, and if I timed it right, I would hear the bells as I walked to lunch. There was something almost magical in the melody of those bells, the sound bouncing from one corner of Mississippi's capital city to the next. If you were paying attention, you could see folks on the street, usually so hurried to get to their destination, briefly lightening their step to hear each glorious note.

In the late spring of 2017, another sound pierced the morning air. Upon hearing that her six-year-old son had been murdered, a young mother wailed as she was carried down the stairs of the Jackson District Attorney's Office. There is a guttural scream a woman makes when she learns her child has died. It comes from deep within; grief enfolds her, and you can hear her heart breaking at the unimaginable loss. Her pain is palpable.

I didn't hear the bells that day.

Mississippi has a violent past, one it's still grappling with. For decades, state officials and historians worked with Mississippians to tell the raw, unfiltered story of Black Mississippians during the civil rights movement. While other museums chronicling the movement exist, our museum was the first in the nation to be state-funded.

Visitors from all over the world have since toured the museum; they move somberly through, astounded at the inflicted horror. I've listened as Hezekiah Watkins tells of the violence he experienced firsthand as the youngest Freedom Rider. With each telling, his voice is strong and powerful, and listeners sit enraptured.

Walking through the museum is emotional, compelling and completely devastating. Yet for all the work done to document what happened here, Mississippi's flag still waved over the Capitol Building just a few blocks away, the Confederate Stars and Bars prominent in the left-hand corner. While reckoning with our past, it was still very much a part of our present.

That flag was voted down by the state legislature in 2020, and Mississippians overwhelmingly voted in favor of a new flag that fall. But to this day, images of the Confederate flag are still painted on the walls of our state capitol.

Former governor Phil Bryant once told me that he believed in the "*Mississippi Burning* effect": people who had never visited our state had very strong opinions about who we were and who we are now based on the 1998 movie that depicted the murder of civil rights activists during the 1960s. Mississippi has tried to move away from that image, but a look through these chapters shows that our past is never truly that far behind us.

For all our wonderful qualities—and yes, there are many—there was once an evil here. As Mississippians, we must acknowledge those evils as we try to move forward toward progress. But sometimes, despite our best efforts, the darkness envelops us.

In the following pages, Ryan and Josh offer a thoughtful, comprehensive look into more than a dozen instances throughout Mississippi's past, ranging from the oddly perverse to crimes so violent they must surely be maleficent. It asks a question: Can Mississippi ever really outrun who it once was? And how far removed are any of us from the devil on the other side of the door?

—Sarah Fowler

PRIDE

....

Every proud man is an abomination to the LORD;
I assure you that he will not go unpunished.
—Proverbs 16:5

And the sin of Pride
has ruined not only me but all my house,
dragging them with it to calamity.
This weight which I refused while I still lived,
I now am forced to bear among the dead,
until the day that God is satisfied.
—Dante, Purgatorio XI, *67–72*

Chapter 1

FINAL FAILURE

The PoFolks Sniper Attack of 1996

*L*arry Wayne Shoemake was distraught. The weight of his accumulated failures had deranged him. He was not thinking straight. Shoemake wrote out the succinct, cryptic note: "I say: separation or annihilation! Who is crazy, me or you? We will see." The note would join his others—read together, they would impress his desire to live in an "all-white society."

If I could just have…all-white…

Fragmented thoughts blinking in an addled mind.

It would all turn good…if…all-white…

Hitler…productive…ALL…WHITE…

Shoemake looked at his bed, a *Reichskriegsflagge* drawn neatly over it. His mother's Bible and a copy of *Mein Kampf* were placed on top. The flag—red, with a black-and-white cross and swastika—would send a clear message when police arrived—perhaps a clearer message than his meager, disjointed writings.

He had been a good writer as a student at Central High School, he believed. That seemed like so long ago. The flag—along with his copy of *Mein Kampf*, his shrine to Waco, his copy of *The Turner Diaries*, his notes—they would explain why it was necessary that Shoemake slaughter Black people in South Jackson and ignite the inevitable race war.[1]

SHOEMAKE PARKED HIS '66 Chevy pickup at the boarded-up PoFolks. The restaurant had offered "hearty homestyle cooking"—chicken, shrimp, "kuntry fried steak"—to residents of South Jackson. But the business had failed, and the vacant restaurant would soon serve a new purpose.[2] He would need to get his guns and ammunition inside the building without raising suspicion. He pried open the back door.

Shoemake kept dozens of guns in his house, all displayed along a wall. He also kept twenty thousand rounds of ammunition. He even had a hand grenade. He had not been able to transport them all to PoFolks. He had carefully selected a few killing instruments.

He unloaded two wooden ammunition crates, maneuvering them toward the building. He unloaded three AK-47s—Russian made, prized for reliability. And then his Colt AR-15—American made, lighter, more accurate. Each held thirty rounds in its long, wide magazine. He unloaded his MAC-11, a stubby machine gun that would discharge its thirty-two rounds, spasmodically, in a few seconds. He unloaded a pump-action twelve-gauge shotgun and a small, personal weapon, his .357 revolver.[3]

He managed to get all his guns and all his ammunition into the PoFolks undetected. The restaurant, though abandoned, sat at the busy intersection of Raymond Road and Ellis Avenue. The building's windows would allow him to fire at Black people from the south, west and north.

From the west-facing window, he could pick off motorists traveling along Ellis Avenue or fire at diners enjoying ice cream at Dairy Queen. From the north-facing window, he could snipe at the cluster of businesses across I-55: Ramada, the BP station, Denny's, Best Western, Days Inn, Burger King—all high-population targets. From the south-facing window, he could fire right into the Pizza Hut next door.

He had failed at most everything he had ever tried. But finally, now, he would become "somebody."[4]

Larry Wayne Shoemake. *Josh Foreman.*

Around 6:00 p.m.

Adrian Vance sat at the red light on Ellis Avenue, waiting to turn right into the Sack and Save grocery store parking lot. To her right was the boarded-up PoFolks. The building was just scenery right until a bullet punched through her windshield.

At the same time, Johnny Hoover Jr. was pulling out of the Sack and Save parking lot onto Ellis Avenue. He heard gunshots and then saw bullets bouncing off the street. Two bullets punched into his car. He saw a pedestrian run and fall. Hoover fled from his car, running, luckily, to safety.

Vance had the presence of mind to pull her three-year-old daughter out of the car and crawl toward the side of the road. With bullets flying overhead, she crawled methodically away from the PoFolks, shielding her daughter with her body. It took her an hour, crawling even after the gunfire had stopped, but she made it three hundred yards to the I-20 interchange, where she sheltered in a drainage ditch.

Hoover jumped from his car and ran away from the PoFolks, escaping to safety.

D.Q. Holifield, too, sat at the Ellis Avenue intersection that afternoon. Holifield, fifty-one, lived in Forest, where he worked as a chicken plant truck driver. His birthday was coming up, and he wanted to make the rare trip to Jackson to buy some new boots and shirts for the party his wife was planning for him. He had taken his son, Johnny. They had done their shopping and were heading back east to Forest. Holifield had missed the I-20 exit and sat stuck in traffic on Ellis Avenue.

When he heard a loud sound, he assumed that his black Cadillac had blown a tire. He stopped, right in front of the PoFolks, and stepped out. Shoemake shot him down in front of his son. When Johnny saw his father fall, bloody, he dropped to a crouch and began running. Johnny was also shot but managed to escape.

Two marines who happened to be in the area rushed toward D.Q. Holifield, with bullets flying all around. They tried to administer first aid. As the marines worked, Shoemake took aim again, shooting D.Q. Holifield again, repeatedly. With the last of his life force, he yelled at the marines, "Run! Save yourselves."[5]

SERGEANT STEVE RENFROE HEARD an alert and looked down at his pager. Something big was happening in South Jackson. This was the kind of thing

Central High School, the all-white high school in Jackson that Larry Wayne Shoemake attended. Image from the school's 1934 *Cotton Boll* yearbook. *Internet Archive.*

Renfroe lived for. "A good felony gets my blood going," he would tell a reporter. "That is what being a police officer is all about."

He hurried toward Ellis Avenue. Renfroe wasn't familiar enough with the area to know that PoFolks had closed recently. When he arrived, he beheld an unimaginable scene. It was pandemonium, and it seemed to be emanating from the PoFolks. Renfroe heard the rapid *pops* of rifle fire and—simultaneously—the *thunks* of 7.62 rounds punching through sheet metal, burying themselves into engine blocks.

For the first time in his nearly twenty-year career as a Jackson police officer, he felt scared. Renfroe, who in photos wore an expressionless face and piercing eyes, imagined the kitchen staff, the diners inside—thought about them lying on the floor, dead or injured.

Renfroe watched police officers from around Jackson—his JPD peers, sheriff's deputies, highway patrolmen, even a Hinds County constable—use their cars to create makeshift barricades. The cars were quickly becoming perforated. Citizens hid behind the cars or behind their own vehicles. Other cops shepherded people away from the scene, likely aware that their body armor could not stop a round from a Kalashnikov.

The chaos lasted for a few minutes after Renfroe's arrival. Sometime during that period, Renfroe realized that the restaurant had been closed—there were no diners or kitchen staff inside. The realization steeled him, and his fear lifted. Renfroe was a member of the SWAT team and, as he liked to say, "heavily armed and equipped to deal with high risk felony situations."[6]

"Time to go to work," he told himself.

PAMELA BERRY, TWENTY-SIX, HAD been with the *Clarion-Ledger* for about a year. The young woman had a lot going on—she was finishing a communication degree at Jackson State University, and she had just gotten married.

She had been sitting in the *Clarion-Ledger* newsroom Friday afternoon when she heard reports of a shooter at PoFolks on her police scanner. She hurried there, parking at the Best Western motel about a half mile north of the restaurant.

She looked toward the restaurant, noticing another journalist, a photographer, much closer to the scene. The photographer was positioned underneath the 1-20 overpass. "I'm not getting that close," she thought. "The Best Western is close enough."

As the magnitude of the situation dawned on Berry, she dialed her colleague's number. Jay Hughes picked up and listened as Berry described the scene.

Berry had no idea that Shoemake had aimed one of his rifles at her. When he unloaded one of the rifle's thirty-round magazines, Jay Hughes listened as bullets struck all around Berry. All thirty rounds would have struck within a few seconds of each other. Hughes listened as one rifle round entered Berry's neck and exited her back.[7]

Berry felt blood pouring down her back and stumbled into the Best Western. A nurse happened to be there, just inside. She guided Berry into a conference room and pressed towels into her neck to keep her from bleeding to death.

Berry asked a man in the lobby to call her parents and her husband. "Just tell them I'm hurt but I'm OK," she said. But she did not believe that everything would be okay. "If I don't make it, tell him I love him," she said, crying.

An ambulance arrived and took Pam to the hospital. She underwent emergency surgery and awoke with her husband snoring by her side. She knew then that she'd survive.[8]

SHOEMAKE'S FIFTY-THREE YEARS OF life up to that point had been a series of personal failures. The son of a World War II veteran, he had dropped out of high school to join the army and fight in Vietnam. He had seemed "bright and full of potential" but returned to the United States and began, as he wrote in an unsent letter, "sliding down…sliding for a long time."

Shoemake married at age twenty. He beat his wife, and within a few years she filed for divorce. He married again. That marriage lasted two years. He married a third time. Again, it ended in divorce. That he could convince three women to marry him proved life's potential—maybe things could have worked out. Three divorces proved his failure—the erasure of potential.

He worked a few low-level jobs and as a drugstore employee and ETV cameraman. But mostly he loafed, shirking life's demands. He used alcohol and drugs. He read.

"He wouldn't work," his third wife would tell a reporter. "I couldn't keep supporting him."

In 1988, he landed a bit part in the 1988 film *Mississippi Burning*. In the film, he helped carry the murdered civil rights workers. The film role stoked a putrid hope inside Shoemake—perhaps the role would lead to stardom; perhaps he would become the "somebody" he felt he deserved to be. *I am somebody. I was born a very special person*!

He read a novel called *The Turner Diaries* around the same time. In the novel, a veteran ignites a race war—whites ultimately annihilate all other races. The novel reaffirmed his racist views and presented Shoemake with a fantasy that would lodge in his mind. His third wife told a reporter that he was never the same after reading *The Turner Diaries*.

When Shoemake's third wife left him around 1989, citing his metastasizing racism, he moved in with his mother at Wingfield Drive in South Jackson. His views had caused other members of his family to avoid him, but his mother took him in, cooking for him and taking care of him. He entered his fifth decade of life with little to show for himself—no career success, broken marriages and no children (at least none whom he had any relationship with; one article mentioned a son from his first marriage). He was a loafer who could not even feed himself, while paradoxically seeing himself as a member of a superior race.

He continued to read and began stockpiling weapons and ammunition. His mother died in 1994. He had nothing left.

BEFORE SHOEMAKE'S ATTACK, HE was arrested in Jackson for drunk driving and drug possession. His mug shot shows a man starved in body and spirit—his mouth hangs open, teeth bared, in a slack, silent scream. Downturned eyes plead for an end to suffering. His hair is a dead man's hair that has continued to grow after burial in a dusty, dry, dark tomb.[9]

Shoemake's attack lasted about forty minutes. During that time, he fired some 1,200 rounds, the metal casings falling to the restaurant floor and gasoline fumes mixing with the smell of spent gunpowder. Shoemake moved, shooting, from south to east to west.

After forty minutes, he set fire to the gasoline he had poured out inside the restaurant. A conflagration began. Shoemake stopped firing and placed his .357 revolver against his temple. A final *pop*.

His rampage wounded ten and killed one: D.Q. Holifield.

The attack had destroyed the peace of South Jackson. But Charlie Smith, the crime scene investigator, wondered why more people had not been killed. "He could have killed at least 25 people," Smith told a reporter. "But I don't think he wanted to kill anybody else."[10]

In the end, it was in character for Shoemake. He had failed again, this time at mass murder. His attack did not ignite a race war.

Chapter 2

PETIT GOD

The Rebirth and Destruction
of a "Cocky Little Man"

Madison County
May 1983

Night fell, and Edward Cates's Honda glowed like a flare. Another driver on Bozeman Road that Saturday night saw the flames. They seemed particularly fierce.

When police arrived, they learned that Cates—a pillar of Jackson society—had been destroyed, along with his vehicle. "Burned to a crisp," the Madison County coroner told a reporter. There was nothing left of him but a leg and torso. The family identified him by a partially burned shoe. An autopsy would reveal that Cates had been alive during the conflagration. Smoke had blackened his lungs. It was a terrible end to a public servant's life.[11]

How could this have happened? The coroner shared his theory. Cates had been in a fender-bender a few days before; the accident must have jostled a gasoline can that Cates kept in the car. Gas had seeped into the floorboards. The car had filled with fumes. A spark from the engine had somehow ignited the spilled gas. The whole thing happened so quickly that Cates could not even open his door and bail out—something he had done many times as a parachuter.

No foul play was suspected, a highway patrol spokesman told reporters. They would continue to investigate, he said. Some questions had not yet been answered, such as why several rubber tires had been piled in the car. Or why there had been so much gasoline spilled before the fateful spark ignited.

Mississippians were informed of Cates's death on Monday in a front-page story in the *Clarion-Ledger*. Cates smiled from above the fold. Readers studied his portrait: he wore a suit and tie and looked to the side with kind, downturned eyes; an authentic, toothy smile; and dark, wavy hair pomaded and combed over.

Cates's obituary listed his accomplishments. He earned degrees from Millsaps, Ole Miss and the University of Maryland. He practiced law in Jackson for decades. He served in the Korean War and eventually attained the rank of brigadier general in the U.S. Army. He was the Jackson city commissioner from 1969 to 1973. He was an assistant state attorney general. He was a deacon at First Presbyterian in Jackson for twenty-one years.

Cates received a military funeral at Lakewood Memorial Cemetery the following day.

AROUND THE SAME TIME, a man shopped for apartments in the Atlanta suburbs. He wanted something inconspicuous but nice. He didn't need the whole apartment to himself; one bedroom in a three-bedroom unit would do.

He picked a unit in Lawrenceville. It was brand-new, cedar-paneled. He told the apartment manager that he was a Vietnam veteran who had been injured and was being forced to retire.

He didn't bring much with him—just his guns, a travel bag, a bedroll and his paratrooper helmet. He moved in a bed and a TV. And, of course, he brought his prescriptions. He took Librium, a powerful, addictive benzodiazepine that blankets the user in a sense of calm, and a medication for his high blood pressure.

He found a running route he liked. He took his fitness seriously, running as much as six miles a day. He found a job—he would sell vacuum cleaners door to door. He had already obtained a display model and a list of potential clients. He introduced himself to his neighbors. "Curts" was his name, he said, although they mostly just called him "the General."[12]

EDWARD CATES'S NEW LIFE as a retired general named Christopher Curts lasted less than a month. At dawn on June 9, 1983, two Mississippi police officers knocked on Cates's apartment door in Lawrenceville, twenty-six days after his charred remains were supposedly found in Madison County.

His arrest begged an important question: if he did not die in the auto fire, whose remains were buried in a flag-draped coffin at Lakewood Memorial?

Who had died an agonizing death in Cates's 1974 Honda Civic, sucking in smoke as the flames leaped around him? Investigators would try to answer that question for the next year, with no help from Cates.

Cates had given himself away almost immediately after faking his death. On the same day of his funeral, Cates's wife, Dorothy, received from "Christopher E. Curts, a retired major general," a Western Union money order for $1,000. "Just heard about Chic's tragedy," an accompanying telegram said. "Am very sorry as he was the best." The telegram promised that a letter would be forthcoming and advised Dorothy Cates not to take any legal action until she had received the letter.[13]

Ed Cates. *Josh Foreman.*

More money orders followed. Dorothy Cates apparently had no inclination that her husband might still be alive. The nickname the major general had used in the telegram, "Chic," was unfamiliar to her, as was the name of the general himself. Confused, she handed the money orders and telegram over to her attorney, who alerted investigators.[14]

When investigators visited the Cates home in Jackson, they found that his travel bag, shaving kit and personal records were gone. They also discovered that he had taken out three life insurance policies in the previous months, totaling $750,000. When they looked for a "Christopher Curts" in army records, they couldn't find one.[15]

As Cates's plot unraveled, police in Jackson began investigating the embezzlement of $223,000 from the Hinds County Co-op in Raymond. The co-op was Cates's client. Investigators discovered that Cates withdrew the sum from the co-op's account, which he controlled through a trust. He then spent the money over a period of four and a half months, writing a "multitude of checks," including a contribution to a local church.[16]

When police arrested him in Lawrenceville, they discovered $28,000 in cash in his sparsely furnished apartment. Cates was formally charged with embezzlement, arson and capital murder, which carried a potential death sentence. He was returned to Mississippi in shackles on June 10, 1983.[17]

Cates's friends and acquaintances could not believe that the man who seemed to have everything squared away could "cave in" so spectacularly.

As reporters looked into his past, clues began to emerge that Cates had not always been the "model citizen" that many perceived him to be.

He was "rabidly ambitious," as one story described him, taking on the trappings of military office before he had attained them; he wore "full-colonel eagles" while still a lieutenant colonel and general's stars while still a colonel. He had clashed with his superiors in the Army Reserve when another officer was promoted over him. Cates said that his competitor was too fat to be in the reserve and demanded that he be expelled. He had delinquent debts and liens. A judge had reprimanded him for unethical conduct during a loan closing.[18]

As a prisoner in Madison County, Cates pleaded innocent to all charges. He remained tight-lipped, refusing to speak to any reporters other than one from the *Los Angeles Times*. During the interview, Cates refused to discuss his case, only saying that he had a "solid defense."[19]

Investigators had plentiful circumstantial evidence against Cates, but key questions remained unanswered. Cates was involved in a shady business deal in the months leading up to him faking his death. Cates, who sometimes bought and sold cars as a side business, purchased five new Cadillacs from a dealer in New Orleans. He then sold them to a dealer in Jackson for a $25,000 loss. Investigators suspected that the deal might be connected to the murder plot.

Most frustratingly, investigators could not discover the identity of the man burned alive in Cates's car. About one month after the body was buried, authorities exhumed it and flew it to Jacksonville, Florida, where Dr. Peter Lipkovic helped examine it. Lipkovic, the forensic pathologist who had helped solve the Ted Bundy murder case, said that he did not have much to go on; all dental records had been destroyed. He hoped that he could match the body to a missing person in Mississippi. Police got several missing person reports, but nothing checked out.[20]

Prosecutors were sure that Cates was at the center of the murder but worried that they could not prove conclusively that he was responsible for the victim's death. It turned out that Edward Cates did not want to risk it.

With his trial for capital murder approaching in January 1984, Cates finally spoke. He didn't reveal whose remains were burned in his Honda the previous May, but he did admit to causing the death of "John Doe."

"Did you on or about May 14, 1983, cause the death of a human being known as John Doe?" Madison County circuit judge Robert Goza asked Cates.

"Yes, sir, I did," Cates replied.

Judge Goza did not ask him further questions about the details of the incident.

Cates pleaded guilty to manslaughter. The plea bargain would save him from a possible death sentence. Shortly after, Cates pleaded guilty to embezzlement. Cates was sentenced to a total of forty years. He would be eligible for parole in ten.[21]

While a prisoner in Madison County, Cates had the "run of the jail," one newspaper story reported. He seemed to enjoy the protection of Madison County sheriff Billy Noble, who allowed him to answer the phone at the jail, jog and eat at local restaurants.

As a state prisoner at Parchman Farm in Sunflower County, however, Cates would enjoy no special treatment. Noble helped protect Cates from state custody. "There ain't no room for him at Parchman," Noble told a reporter.

But others felt strongly that Cates should be transferred to Parchman. After fighting for months to avoid it, Cates was finally taken from the Madison County Jail in May 1984 and driven to Parchman.

Thus ended the media spectacle that had surrounded the Cates case for the previous year. Cates spent the next six years living the life of a common prisoner at Parchman. On December 2, 1990, he died of a heart attack in his cell.

IN THE AFTERMATH OF Cates's plea, the police who investigated his case were left only with theories and unanswered questions. Bob Campbell, one of the two Mississippi officers who had arrested Cates in Lawrenceville, was convinced that Cates had picked up a drifter in New Orleans, promised him an opportunity in Jackson, drugged him or got him drunk and set him on fire that night on Bozeman Road in Madison County.

Cates spent a "great deal of time" in New Orleans in the months leading to his plot. "You can get lost easy there," Campbell told a reporter. "I think he had some reason to go there."

Campbell told a reporter that Cates was a "cocky little man" and that the media attention had made him feel, "Hey, I'm somebody."[22]

Cates's yearbook photos from the University of Mississippi hint at the duality of the man. In his 1948 photo, Cates wears a broad, toothy smile and looks into the camera with friendly, unguarded eyes. His 1951 photo shows a different person; Cates stares past the camera with suspicion, his mouth set firm with no hint of a smile.[23]

Ed Cates's 1952 Ole Miss yearbook photo (*second row, leftmost photo*). *Internet Archive.*

They are the faces of a prideful man. Cates thought a lot of himself and wanted others to think a lot of him too. When he made a donation to a local church with stolen money, his motive was to appear caring. But he ultimately cared so little for others that his lack of care turned to scorn.

Cates acted as a petit god, able to erase one person and create another. But in the end, the few embarrassed mourners at his funeral—his *actual* funeral—saw what he really was: a fallen and unrepentant sinner who made the world a worse place.

Chapter 3

JAMES JACKSON SR.

The "Three Minute Man"

Rankin County Jail
1987

James Jackson lugged the heavy computer to his workspace. He planned to spend a few hours repairing the hard drive and software. Then he would haul the repaired machinery back to the District Attorney's Office. He was grateful for the labor, both physical and mental. Soon it would be the weekend and his son would pick him up and take him "home" for the weekend.

At 9:00 p.m., James received a request from the sheriff's office asking him to escort a young legal assistant assigned to work on bad check research to her car. James acquiesced and met the woman at the back door. She thanked him, and he introduced himself: "I'm James Jackson."

Terrified, the young lady put one foot in front of the next until she and her escort reached her car. Politely, the "best damn warden…in the Rankin County jail up to that time" bid her adieu and returned to his jail cell.

Still shaking, Sharon Jernigan drove home and informed her husband, Al, that she had been escorted to her car by the man Al helped put in jail for murdering his wife just a year before.[24]

Columbia, Mississippi
March 12, 1985, 8:56 p.m.

James Jackson calmly stood, looking down at his wife, careful not to let the expanding pool of blood stain his shoes. She lay face down in her own blood, a gaping wound filled with glass shards in the back of her skull. A broken Coca-Cola bottle lay shattered around her. She was still breathing but beginning to choke on her blood. Jackson walked to his office, picked up a phone and called the police.

James Jackson. *Josh Foreman.*

"This is James Jackson at the Red Carpet Motors. We've been robbed. My wife is hurt bad. I need an ambulance."[25]

Within two minutes, the first officer arrived. He walked through the showroom and into the office, where he noticed blood splattered on the wall and Jackson squatting over his wife. He looked impeccable in his stylish clothes and fancy shoes. Mary Nell lay beneath him, slowly bleeding to death.

Jackson calmly walked into another office to place a phone call. Moments later, he left the office and coolly walked to the ambulance that was ready to rush his dying wife to the hospital. Jackson locked the office behind him and followed behind the stretcher carrying his wife. Rather than ride with her in the back of the ambulance, Jackson passed her by to sit up front. Once at the hospital, as doctors tried in vain to save his wife's life, Jackson met with a police officer to once again go over what was stolen during the robbery—most notably personal effects and a Red Carpet Motors blue money bag.

James Jackson drove home, knowing that he had beat the system yet again.

1967

Jackson knew that his people skills and intelligence put him above the law. It always did. Back in 1967, he was charged with four years of tax evasion. He pleaded no contest and accepted a $6,000 fine but had his jail sentence suspended. Confident that he would quickly earn that $6,000 back, Jackson moved his wife, Mary Nell, and son, Jimmy, from Hattiesburg to Columbia. Having worked the previous fifteen years at a Chevrolet dealership, Jackson began working at his brother-in-law's Chevrolet business. Soon thereafter, he bought the dealership.

James and Mary Nell found a house that they bought for $25,000. After renovating their new home, they insured it for $60,000. Not long after, the fire department arrived to investigate the scent of gas filling the house. The gas valve next to the fireplace had been purposefully left open. All the windows and doors were locked. Later, the fire department returned to Jackson's house to investigate another gas leak. Once again, gas had been allowed to permeate the house when no one was at home. There was no sign of forced entry. Finally, on September 10, 1971, an explosion rocked the Jackson house. The fire marshal determined that a gas valve had been opened in the attic, where a lighted candle had been left. Again, there was no sign of forced entry, and all the windows and doors were locked.

Mary Nell and Jimmy both gave statements to investigators, but James refused. Initially all three agreed to a polygraph test, but James soon after canceled under the advice of his lawyer.

No charges were pressed, and the Jacksons soon purchased a new home in a wealthier section of town. District Attorney Richard Douglass claimed, "Jackson's success with the arson incident showed his predilection to break the law in order to get what he wanted, and it strengthened his belief that he could beat the system."[26]

Mary Jackson, based on an image that was published after her murder. *Josh Foreman.*

JAMES JACKSON QUICKLY BECAME a well-respected member of Columbia. He joined First Baptist Church, where he sang each Sunday in the choir. He had a nice house, owned a car dealership and accumulated a devoted group of admirers. He had a wife who was even more beloved by his church family, always smiling, warm and friendly.

Jackson had entirely ingratiated himself to the Columbia community. On both sides of town.

JACKSON TOOK EXTREME PRIDE in his appearance. Standing more than six feet tall, pale and with a dark-brown receding hairline and angular face, he wore dark-rimmed glasses over his dark-brown eyes. He was always well-dressed, even dapper. His trim appearance lent him credibility among his customers, respectability among his fellow Baptists and an air of affluence when in the presence of his "mistress."[27]

James Jackson was living a double life. The choirboy had a mistress on the side—an African American drug user and prostitute,[28] far removed from First Baptist Church of Columbia society. An interracial affair—and by a member of First Baptist's choir—would have permanently destroyed Jackson's image and standing in Columbia. It didn't matter; he was too clever to get caught. The affair went on for months undetected.

Red Carpet Motors
Columbia, Mississippi
March 12, 1985

Having just gotten off the phone with her friend Muriel, Mary Nell stood up for the final time. A Coke bottle slammed into her head, filling it with glass shrapnel. She never regained consciousness. Before the next day ended, Mary Nell Jackson was dead.

James Jackson calmly accompanied his wife to the hospital. While there, he told investigators that he didn't know what had happened because he was in another room being robbed. Among the items the robber stole was a blue bank bag full of money.

Jackson's bookkeeper, Lynn Meadows, who had rushed to the hospital to be with Mary Nell, overheard her boss's report.

March 13

After a traumatic night at the hospital, Meadows received a call from Jackson's son, Jimmy, asking her to locate some workers compensation forms. She drove to Red Carpet Motors and began looking in the file cabinets for the requested forms. A bag fell to the floor. A blue bank bag—full of checks from March 12.

Terrified, knowing that a killer was on the loose and that she might be next, she dropped the money bag back in the file cabinet and told neither the police nor any one at the dealership.

March 15
The Day of Mary Nell's Funeral

Having finally been told by his wife, who was still scared senseless, Sonny Meadows called the chief of police and told him that his men had missed a valuable piece of evidence at the dealership. Joe Sanders and Carroll Bryant once again searched the business. This time, when Bryant entered the computer room, he found a blue money bag in the bottom of a file cabinet.

Some of the receipts were dated March 12, the night of the murder.

UNABLE TO LOCATE ANY reasonable suspects, investigator Carroll Bryant and Police Chief Joe Sanders asked Jackson to put down on paper *all* he remembered of that night. Jackson confidently went home and typed out the following statement:

> *After I was attempting the open safe, for a few minutes, I heard a noise in the back (In shop area). It was not a scream, or I did not hear anyone talking, It just sounded like something fell. Like several things fell. I attempted to leave the safe and investigate the noise, and I was struck on the head with the gun that the party was holding on me....As I handed him the bag, he said give me your rings and I took them off my fingers and handed them to him, he then jerked my watch off my arm. He then said give me all of your money. I reached into my left front pants pocket and got my money folder. (A leather folder just for bills) and gave it to him. He then turned to run out, and I started to run after him. He stopped about the back door and pointed the Gun at me, and said you stay right there, and don't follow me....I stopped for just a minute, and then as he was gone I went into the shop.... Then my eyes fell on my wife who was lying on the floor face down, and you could begin to see blood running from underneath her. I stopped for just a split second, and could tell she was breathing, and was alive, altho not moving at all. I then ran into the service manager office, and dialed 911. Told them who I was and where I was, that we had been robbed and my wife was hurt bad, to send the Police and an ambulance.*[29]

No doubt James Jackson slept well that night, knowing his typed statement had put the case to rest. The murder of his wife, Mary Nell Jackson, would forever remain a cold case.

Red Carpet Motors
Tuesday, April 2, 1985, 8:30 p.m.

By now, District Attorney Richard Douglass had begun to suspect Jackson of murdering his wife. His behavior was inconsistent with a grieving husband, and his story was full of holes, if not lies. With no witnesses present, Richard Douglass determined that he must prove to the jury that Jackson's written statement was implausible. And so, he took a huge gamble. He asked Jackson to produce a reenactment of the murder via video.

Jackson would be given complete control over the filming. He had already written the script. Now he would cast, act and direct in his own production. He would star in a movie centered on the traumatic death of his wife. And he would play the bad guy.

Jackson cast his own son, Jimmy, to play the role of himself. Jackson would play the vault robber. His wife and the other robber would be left off screen. The investigators helped Jackson arrange the set exactly as it had been on the night of March 12. The cars were where they had been, and the filming would begin at the same time of night so as to replicate the lighting at that time of evening. The camera would follow Jimmy (playing his father) so as to mimic James Jackson's movements that night. Jackson was reminded one last time that he was in charge—he may stop or edit as he pleased. He may even refuse to cooperate as the tape may or may not be played in court.

An excited and confident Jackson agreed to proceed as he donned his robbers' gear: a ski mask, long-sleeved shirt, leather gloves and revolver. The crew began to arrive at 7:30 p.m. By 8:30 p.m., they were ready to roll. At 8:35 p.m., filming began:

[from the camera's perspective]

Nothing.
  After a second attempt rattling the garage doors, banging can be heard.
  Jimmy, rising to investigate, goes into the garage where he sees a man at the front doors wearing a ski mask. He shouts, "Can I help you?"
  The masked man raises a gun and replies, "You can open the safe and give me the money."
  A compliant Jimmy leads the armed robber to the shop doors, opens them and walks down the hall to the safe where the two squat down. In conformity with the script, Jimmy twice fails to enter the correct combination.

The camera's microphone picks up the sound of two bottles shattering in the background.

Jimmy tries to go to the office where the bottles broke but is struck on the head by the robber's gun. "If you don't open the safe, I will kill you!"

On the third try, Jimmy opens the safe and hands the money bag to the robber, who promptly asks for Jimmy's two rings. The robber has difficulty holding the gun in one hand, the money bag, and now the rings in the other. Nevertheless, he now tries to rip the watch off Jimmy's wrist (according to the script). After several failed attempts, Jimmy has to take off the watch himself and hand it to the robber who then asked for his money clip as well. Unable to hold everything, the robber drops some items, including his gun.

The robber gathers his items, and runs to the garage door, and departs. The scene ends.[30]

A smug James Jackson took off his mask, pleased with his performance. Given the chance to edit or redo any scene, he declined, claiming to be satisfied.

He then went outside, where he noticed District Attorney Douglass standing by his car. James approached the prosecutor and extended his hand. Having just relived the most tragic event of his life—the brutal murder of his wife—James was in good spirits. The DA was in a position to help him. With the murder unsolved and the killer on the loose, James had an important question: he had repaired a customer's vehicle, and now the customer refused to pay. How could he collect his money?

ACCORDING TO JAMES JACKSON, the robber first rattled the doors of his dealership at 8:35 p.m. He made his tranquil 911 call at 8:56 p.m., twenty-one minutes later. The reenactment he had been so pleased with had lasted four minutes and thirteen seconds.[31]

CONVINCED THAT JAMES JACKSON was a liar and just as convinced that his pride would bring him down, the DA decided to seek an indictment. In his mind, the case was simple. Two people entered Red Carpet Motors on March 12, 1985. One ended up murdered. The other emerged with a fabricated story that simply did not make sense. There was no doubt in Richard Douglass's mind that James Jackson was the murderer.

On July 16, 1985, a Marion County Grand Jury agreed with Douglass and indicted James Jackson for the murder of his wife.[32]

THE TRIAL OF JAMES Jackson for the murder of his wife, Mary Nell, would rock and split the Columbia community. Supporters of Jackson stood by him throughout the process, filling the courtroom during the trial. Just as many, eventually convinced of his guilt, turned their back on the former deacon. Everyone had an opinion. District Attorney Richard Douglass later claimed, "He gave to all kinds of charities in town. A lot of people didn't know this, but when he moved to [Columbia] from Hattiesburg, he had four federal convictions for tax evasion. Law enforcement had also already looked at a fire he had at his house, and it was ruled arson. They couldn't prove he did it."[33]

After all, James Jackson was a respected member of the community. He ran a successful business. He gave generously to charities. He sang in the church choir. He also had a mistress on the side. He also had a checkered past. He also had treated his wife's death so callously.

Everyone in Columbia had an opinion of James Jackson.

March 14, 1986

The trial went as trials go, with the ebb and flow of accusation and defense, the presentation and refutation of evidence, the constant jury watching to see which arguments scored points. At last, the time for final arguments arrived. Then came a surprise: James Jackson decided to represent himself in closing arguments. Confident that only he could be his salvation and that his ability and intelligence would win his acquittal, Jackson arose to determine his own fate.

Richard Douglass related what happened next:

> *James Jackson stood before the jury in his suit and yellow legal pad. He had the look of a lawyer or maybe a preacher. I correlate the two, hoping I am not insulting either. The courtroom was not Jackson's platform of preference, but he liked public attention, and he spoke with his own brand of charisma, salesmanship, and self-confidence. In the beginning, he spoke without the least tremble in his voice. He delivered his organized speech without hesitation, but Jackson talked in a manner removed from the tragedy of his wife's death. He delivered his summation more in the way of indignant defiance at being unjustly brought before the court.*
>
> *Having sat through the trial all week, James Jackson now had his chance to argue his own fate and was confident that he could sway the jury.*

Why shouldn't James Jackson feel perfectly confident about his chances when he had lived a life of deception?[34]

When the jury returned its verdict, James Jackson's pride was finally shaken. He was sentenced to twenty years for manslaughter.

James Jackson spent the rest of his life in prison. Even there, he won the trust and respect of his guards. Soon he was granted weekend passes to leave and visit his son in Hattiesburg. He always reported back on Sunday. He was free to move about inside the prison and was made the de facto IT man of the jail. Rankin County judge Kent McDaniel claimed, "Jackson was the best damn 'warden' we had in the Rankin County jail up to that time. He 'ran' all the inmate control issues and brought us into at least the 20th century with computers to track inmates."[35]

Between Jackson's parole and his official release, he was given a physical during which he learned that he had contracted an advanced, terminal illness. James Jackson—so confident, so dapper, so proud—died in a hospital, in custody of the state.[36]

ENVY

....

Then the L<small>ORD</small> *said to Cain: Why are you angry? Why are you dejected?*
If you act rightly, you will be accepted; but if not, sin lies in wait at the door: its
urge is for you, yet you can rule over it.
Cain said to his brother Abel, "Let us go out in the field." When they were in
the field, Cain attacked his brother Abel and killed him.
—Genesis 4:6–8

…the eyelids of these shades had been sewn shut
with iron threads, like falcons newly caught,
whose eyes we stitch to tame their restlessness.
—Dante, Purgatorio *XIII, 70–72*

Chapter 4

THE FA(U)LKNERS
AND THEIR RIVALS

Mexico to Ripley, Mississippi
1846–89

The Second Mississippi was under orders to remain in camp. But First Lieutenant William C. Falkner had business in town. He had been visiting the nearby Mexican town whenever he could. His trips had not gone unnoticed.

When Falkner rode by one evening, he was struck by two musket balls, one entering his left foot and the other tearing off the tops of three fingers on his left hand. The wounds were nonlethal but debilitating, and Falkner was forced to apply for a medical discharge. Once granted, the lieutenant returned home to north Mississippi.

Three years later, Falkner's wounds still caused him pain. He applied for a government pension. His wounds, after all, were sustained while serving his country in wartime. He was counting on the pension.

What Falkner did not know was that his former rival, Thomas Hindman, was fighting to block Falkner's pension. He had spread the story that Falkner was not wounded in battle. Instead, he had been shot while disobeying orders.

General Taylor had issued strict orders forbidding his men from visiting the nearby town of Aguas Calientes. But Falkner had been giving his attentions to a young señorita of that town and had no intention to cease his amorous sorties. Neither did his rival.

Whereas Falkner was willing to disobey orders for love, his jealous rival was willing to kill for the same end. The rival, according to Lieutenant Hindman, lay in ambush one night on the road connecting the camp and town. Hindman insisted that it was a combination of a personal vendetta and poor judgment, and not military service, that caused Falkner's wounds.[37]

Falkner was furious. When he saw Thomas's brother, Robert Hindman,[38] on the street, he accosted him. Robert drew a pistol and fired on Falkner, but the pistol misfired. Falkner unsheathed his Bowie knife and plunged it into his rival's brother.

It was determined that Falkner had acted in self-defense, and life went on for the ambitious lawyer and businessman. Two years later, he killed Hindman's good friend Erasmus Norris and again avoided prison when he claimed self-defense.[39]

Falkner's final twenty-seven years passed more peacefully as he dove into politics and expanded his businesses. Along with his partner, Richard Jackson Thurmond, he invested in the Ripley Railroad and made a small fortune. Eventually, the two had a falling out, and Falkner bought Thurmond out. Thurmond's finances waned as Falkner's waxed, leading Thurmond, in a fit of jealous rage, to confront his former partner.

On Tuesday, November 5, 1889, William Falkner stood in Ripley's town square, next to the J.A. Norris and Company General Store and Hotel, talking business with Thomas Rucker. Thurmond approached and drew his .44-caliber pistol. A shocked Falkner cried out, "What do you mean, Dick? Don't shoot." Thurmond fired at point-blank range. He was so close that Rucker received powder burns from the discharge. Falkner received the lethal ball, which entered under his tongue, smashed into his jaw and lodged in his neck just under his right ear. Falkner hit the ground. His son-in-law, Dr. Nathaniel Carter, sat him up and wiped the blood from his face as Falkner groaned, "Dick, what did you do it for?" Hours later, William Falkner was dead at sixty-four.[40]

Mississippi to Cuba to Stockholm, Sweden
1946–61

> *Ernest Hemingway…has no courage, has never crawled out on a limb. He has never been known to use a word that might cause the reader to check with a dictionary to see if it is properly used.*
>
> —*William Faulkner*[41]

Poor Faulkner. Does he really think big emotions come from big words? He thinks I don't know the ten-dollar words. I know them all right. But there are older and simpler and better words, and those are the ones I use. Did you read his last book? It's all sauce-writing now, but he was good once. Before the sauce, when he knew how to handle it.

—*Ernest Hemingway*[42]

While delivering a talk in Oxford, Mississippi, William Faulkner, the great-grandson of William C. Falkner, first lieutenant of the Mississippi Rifles, was asked where he stood among contemporary American writers. He placed himself second, behind Thomas Wolfe. Wolfe had been dead for eight years, so Faulkner was rating himself the greatest living American novelist. Ernest Hemingway was number four on Faulkner's list.

The *New York Herald Tribune* reported Faulkner's address—including his claim that Hemingway had no courage. For the ultra-competitive Hemingway, who had followed Faulkner's career at a distance, the literary gauntlet had been thrown down. The Arthur and Lancelot of American literature would fight for the same damsel: recognition as America's foremost novelist.

The previous year, the senior editor at Random House suggested that Hemingway write the introduction to a Faulkner book soon to be released. Faulkner objected and readily admitted that he considered Hemingway a rival: "I am opposed to asking Hemingway to write the preface. It seems to me in bad taste to ask him to write a preface to my stuff. It's like asking one race horse in the middle of a race to broadcast a blurb on another horse in the same running field."

Most likely, Hemingway was offended, but he was also relieved that he had avoided the odium of contributing to a book in which he played second fiddle to his rival. He wrote, "[Faulkner] has the most talent of anybody and he just needs a sort of conscience that isn't there....But he will write absolutely perfectly straight and then go on and on and not be able to end it."

And thus Hemingway perpetuated the perceived and oft-cited distinction between the two: Faulkner's gregariousness and Hemingway's forthrightness. (As countless professors have often pleaded with their students: "More Hemingway, less Faulkner.") The truth, however, is that the two even competed in sentence construction, from Faulkner's brief and famous "My mother is a fish"[43] to Hemingway's 424-word sentence in *The Green Hills of Africa*.[44] (The latter was topped by Faulkner's 1,288-word sentence in *Absalom, Absalom!*) No doubt, the two distinctive—though overlapping—styles contributed to the rivalry.

Left: William Faulkner by Carl Van Vechten (1954). *Library of Congress.*

Right: Ernest Hemingway in Cuba. *Florida Keys History Center, Monroe County Public Library.*

A letter from Faulkner to "Brother H" in May 1947 seemingly offered a truce. His remarks were not meant for public consumption. He was answering a question without filtering his words. He was not questioning Hemingway's personal courage, but literary. In turn, Hemingway apologized for his retaliatory remarks. He even told Faulkner that he would appreciate his input on his latest novel, *For Whom the Bell Tolls.* He suggested that the two continue to correspond "as brothers."[45]

Faulkner and Hemingway would not speak again, and the joust would resume, each inflicting pain on the other. In 1949, Faulkner severely wounded his challenger when he won the Nobel Prize for Literature. Hemingway returned the blow and won his own Nobel Prize five years later. The year before, in 1953, a distraught Hemingway, who had been excoriated by critics and declared a washout, retaliated with *The Old Man and the Sea.* Not to be outdone, Faulkner won the same award the next year for his novel *A Fable.*

As their final years ebbed away, the two great writers continued to produce, always with an eye on the other's progress and accolades. Unable to bear the strain of their craft and all its concomitant trials—the critics, the lonesomeness, the self-doubt, the rivalries—the two contenders sought solace and peace outside their writing, Hemingway in oblivion and Faulkner in the bottle. The two rivals joined each other in death one year apart, as well as in the pantheon of literary immortals.

Chapter 5

THE BEAUTYBERRY MAFIOSO

Natchez's War for Pilgrimage Supremacy

1932

The Great Schism, the War Between the Garden Clubs, the Great Betrayal, the War of Pilgrimage Club Aggression—this conflict began in the mid-1930s, in the midst of the Great Depression.

In 1930, the allure that was Natchez had been dwindling. Its economy was in decline. Its relevance was waning. Its mansions were in decay. The feudal society that had turned Natchez into the wealthiest antebellum city, renowned for its opulence and mansions, was still strong. The rest of the city was not.

Natchez was run by an aging patriarchy, overseeing a crumbling economy. And then a queen stepped forward, promising an economic and cultural revival: Katherine I of Natchez, Queen of Hope Farm, the former residence of Spanish governor Carlos de Grand-Pre.

Katherine Miller acquired her domain when she promised her husband all the hunting dogs he craved if he bought her the estate she coveted. And so, Hope Farm was transformed into an estate that would be only the beginning of her grand plan.[46] An estate that just might bring back some of the "glory of the old south."

QUEEN KATHERINE I TOOK over Natchez society. She had a plan to revitalize the city, culturally and economically. In the words of Harnett Thomas Kane, "She has the deceptively easy charm of the old time Southern belle, together

"On the Bluff" in Natchez. By H.C. Norman (circa late 1800s). *New York Public Library.*

with a rigid determination to get what she wants. She was, and is, a dramatic lady, who deals in large things, frets over trifles, hates routine and drives everybody, including herself, close to a breakdown."[47] A fellow resident of Natchez claimed that Katherine had fifteen ideas per minute, "thirteen of them ridiculous, two brilliant or something close to it."[48]

Katherine's Hope Farm renovations, along with her social connections and boisterous personality, catapulted her to the presidency of Natchez's premier social club: the Natchez Garden Club. She was determined to revitalize Natchez's failing economy and would do so through the tourism industry—one house at a time.

She convinced the other women of the Natchez Garden Club to renovate and open their antebellum homes to tourists from across the country. Natchez would offer a "pilgrimage of houses." She promised that pilgrims would come, lots of them. It was in the midst of the Great Depression. Still, she guaranteed that they'd come. *If you fix it, they will come.*

Katherine then embarked on a propaganda/marketing campaign to recruit pilgrims from all over the nation. The homeowners spruced up their houses and beautified their gardens. Katherine's ladies mailed invitations, printed notices and contacted papers. They prepared to host a party. They planned a parade. They promised a spectacle.

Then the day of the first Natchez Pilgrimage finally arrived, and Katherine I's prognostications of success were actualized. The pilgrims materialized. So successful was Katherine's Hail Mary that Natchez decided to do it again next year. A Confederate ball was added. And then other balls. And more parades and picnics. Pilgrimage became the social and financial event of the year. And the next. And the next.

Katherine Miller created an economic windfall for the financially insolvent town of Natchez. Natchez soon became the jewel of the South, a tourist destination to compete with Savannah and New Orleans. Nay, it was a *pilgrimage* port of call for all lovers of gardens and mansions.

1935

War was on the horizon—Natchez's second civil war.

Harnett Thomas Kane explained: "Then, 1935, and high-pitched hell broke over Natchez, in what the town has ever afterward called 'the split.' It developed over personalities, principles if you will, and also money—specifically, the take."[49]

The Natchez Garden Club had made more than a handsome profit from its pilgrimage houses. Two-thirds of that money had gone to the homeowners who had borne the expense of maintaining an antebellum home. (Not to mention opening their doors to guests they had never seen before, and many of those from north of the Mason-Dixon line.) Many in the club believed that the remaining one-third of the money Katherine's idea had accrued ought to go to the homeowners so the homes could remain operable. Others wanted the money to go into a community pot so the Natchez Garden Club could add more houses to their registry of "Pilgrimage Houses."

The Natchez Garden Club was split, but it looked as if the latter view would prevail. Katherine was livid.

In June 1936, she led a revolt and took seventeen of the twenty-six Pilgrimage homes with her, opening a rival Pilgrimage under the auspices of the newly formed Natchez Pilgrimage Club.[50]

Katherine Miller had established a rival kingdom. To many, this visionary had solidified herself as Katherine I, Queen of the Pilgrimage. To others, her pride and greed had tarnished her accomplishments. To them, she would henceforth be known as "I, Katherine." The two sides split into bitter, quarrelsome camps.

Eighty-five years later, Natchez resident Kathie Blankenstein explained the consequences of Katherine's defection:

> *Essentially they were mad about money, and they had a big fight and put on separate Pilgrimages. I, Katherine, begged my mother to come over to the new club, but she was loyal and disapproved of what they were doing. As far as she was concerned, I, Katherine, had betrayed the Natchez Garden Club and fallen from grace. Oh, it was terrible. It broke up bridge clubs. It broke up lifelong friendships. My mother and her childhood friends ended up being bitter enemies until they died. And it was maddening. Those women had no loyalty at all! It was just a business to them, and they were social mavens. That's why they went with I, Katherine.*[51]

Longwood in Natchez. *Library of Congress.*

The community was torn asunder. Each club held its own Pilgrimage. Each hosted its own ball. Each crowned its own king and queen. They established rival headquarters: Magnolia Hall for the Natchez Garden Club and Longwood for the Pilgrimage Garden Club. The "War of the Hoopskirts" split Natchez as had the War of the Roses split England five hundred years before.[52]

When one club opened its houses, the other barred its doors. Pulitzer Prize–winning war correspondent Ernie Pyle traveled to Natchez and claimed, "It's the AFL and CIO all over again."[53] The Natchez Garden Club demanded an injunction against the Pilgrimage Garden Club. It got it. The Pilgrimage Garden Club responded by suing the Natchez Garden Club.

Natchez's mayor left town. The judge overhearing the suit pleaded with the ladies to settle their differences: their rivalry and envy were endangering Natchez's Pilgrimage cash cow.[54]

Natchez, Mississippi
1947

The rivals sat around the council table. The war had been going on for a dozen years. The only respite had come when Nazis, Communists and GIs fought a much larger conflict five thousand miles away. That war had only temporarily put the Battle for Pilgrimage on hold.

The brief respite that put Hitler in his grave was now over, and the ladies of Natchez resumed their own battle for social and economic supremacy. But even the war-weary women of Natchez needed a respite. The two sides reached an agreement. There would once again be one royal family, one Confederate Ball, one Pilgrimage.

Mrs. Melchior Beltzhoover, president of the Pilgrimage Garden Club, extended her hand to Mrs. Homer Washington of the Natchez Garden Club. The civil war had finally come to an end.[55]

The lawsuits, the padlocked mansions, the graffiti, the laxatives to rival dogs and more would become just bitter memories.[56]

2020

The Natchez Pilgrimage entered its seventy-third year since the truce. The famed Malaysian-born British writer Richard Grant traveled to Natchez to investigate what he would call "the most southern place of all." Grant had recently published a smashing success of life in the Mississippi Delta.[57] Now he turned his attention and his talents to Natchez. The result was a nearly three-hundred-page book. Much of his manuscript focused on the garden club rivalry.

Natchez icon, "Queen of Biscuits" and Pilgrimage Garden Club president Regina Charboneau took Grant under her wing and introduced the Brit to Natchez, as well as to the quietly ongoing feud between the clubs. Charboneau explained that the Natchez Garden Club was lower class, "poisoned by jealousy and feelings of inferiority."[58]

On the other hand, members of the Natchez Garden Club argued that the Pilgrimage Garden Club was the "bigger, richer, more powerful and aristocratic club"[59] and that its members were "arrogant, divisive, and domineering." In fact, they were called "Pills," as in they were "bitter in the mouth, and hard to swallow."[60] Nancy Hungerford, Natchez Garden Club member and the executive director of Natchez's Children's Services, added, "Sometimes we can't help feeling mad that they took so many of our homes away from us. And the Pills act so snooty sometimes, like *they're* the real garden club, just because they've got more homes and money."[61]

While the two clubs publicly set aside their differences for the sake of Natchez, the friction and envy betwixt the two was obvious to Grant.

2023

The fragile truce between the Natchez Garden Club and Pilgrimage Garden Club was challenged in 2023 when the former decided that it was time for a change. Natchez Garden Club president Donna Sessions explained, "We decided we wanted to begin our own Pilgrimage. We wanted to go in a different direction." Sessions and her ladies took a good many of Natchez's most famous homes with them.

When news of the secession broke, Marsha Colson of the Pilgrimage Garden Club made no official comment other than claiming that the traditional Pilgrimage hosted by the Pilgrimage Garden Club would go on as scheduled and that the homes in her club would open their doors as they had been doing for the previous ninety years.[62]

Not surprisingly, pilgrims were required to buy their tickets in two separate locations: through the Natchez Garden Club or the Natchez Pilgrimage Club. And so the feud continues.

Chapter 6

BOTTOM FEEDERS

River Pirates Take,
When Opportunity Presents Itself

1901

It was a grisly fact of life in Greenville: once in a while, corpses—or "floaters," as people called them—would come drifting down the river. The floaters were drowned men from Tennessee or suicides from Arkansas. Perhaps they were workers who had fallen off a boat, or drunken men. Sometimes they were just corpses, badly decomposed and condemned forever to anonymity.

Greenville's city marshal, William Quinn, would try to discern the identities of these floaters when they came to his city, comparing the bodies' features with reports of missing persons from farther north. Marshal Quinn knew, as he examined a floater on July 14, that this was not a typical case. The corpse bore a telltale sign of foul play: its face had been "battered out of all semblance to humanity," and a heavy iron weight had been tied to its neck.

It didn't take long for Quinn to connect the body to a report of a missing man whose houseboat was found pulled ashore and looted in Arkansas a week before. When Quinn discovered that two unfamiliar men had landed in Greenville on two bateaux the same day the body was discovered—that they had sold a skiff bearing the name "F.W. Vogus" for pennies on the dollar—he knew that he had found the murderers.

Vogus, the murdered man, had been the victim of another sad aspect of life on the Mississippi in those days: river pirates. River pirates were opportunistic drifters who traveled America's rivers looking for easy money. Sometimes the pirates would commit property crimes at an opportune moment, collecting timber, broken loose from its moorings, floating downstream; looting a corpse or a wrecked ship; or stopping at a landing to take cotton bales that had been set there for pickup.

Sometimes the pirates would commit much more heinous crimes, such as the time in 1889 when a gang of eleven men and women, led by an escaped Chicago prisoner named Tommy O'Dowd, overpowered the workers of a stave factory in Cairo, Illinois, blew up their safe and took sixty dollars worth of valuables. Then there was the time two men promised to buy a flatboat off an elderly owner in Natchez—if only they could just get to New Orleans and secure the funds. On the way, they cleaved the old man's head with an axe.[63]

"Highwayman," from the "Occupations for Women" series for Old Judge and Dogs Head Cigarettes (1887). *Metropolitan Museum of Art.*

Quinn began sending telegrams to law enforcement officers down the river. He sent one to Vicksburg—*Be on the lookout for these two; here's what they look like.*

The chief of police in Vicksburg set a watch at the city's lower landing. A day later, the bateaux pulled up at Vicksburg. It wasn't there long, and the two men departed quickly. But they were there long enough for the lookout to telephone the chief of police. The chief organized a party of officers, and they set off down the river after the two. They found them "snugly ensconced in a pocket"—tied up at an island in the river, relaxing. The officers aimed their Winchester rifles at the two white men, one almost seventy and the other just out of his twenties. They didn't resist.

New technologies, the telegraph and the telephone, were proving to be effective tools against piracy; where once river pirates could travel the river faster than the speed of messengers, now communication between cities was instantaneous.

Ultimately, the two men were tried and acquitted—the state, due to lack of witnesses, could not prove that they had committed the murder. Ultimately, despite technological advances, the untamed nature of the river meant that people could still get away with dirty deeds.[64]

WRATH

....

Cease from anger and forsake wrath;
Do not fret; it leads only to evildoing.
—Psalm 37:8

"[F]ix thine eyes below, for draweth near
The river of blood, within which boiling is
Whoe'er by violence doth injure others."
O blind cupidity, O wrath insane,
That spurs us onward so in our short life,
And in the eternal then so badly steeps us!
—Dante, Inferno *XII, 46–51*

Chapter 7

THE CARROLLTON COUNTY
COURTHOUSE MASSACRE

Carrollton, Mississippi
March 17, 1886

Dust filled the air to the west, enough to choke anyone along the road. More than four dozen horsemen galloped toward the Carrollton Courthouse, where the plaintiffs awaited their day of justice. Everyone in the town awaited the outcome of the trial—whites and Blacks, as well as the two mixed Choctaw-Black accusers.

The mixed audience eagerly awaited the presentation of the evidence. More importantly, they awaited the verdict. It would be a judgment that set the tone for race relations in the region for the next generation.

The dust swirled in the air and slowly resettled on the ground as the horsemen dismounted, some heading for the four doors of the courthouse and the rest positioning themselves around the building.

Within minutes, the courtroom would be filled with smoke, choking the men who frantically sought a cover that did not exist.

Mississippi
1865

Shock, denial, disillusionment. Mississippi found itself in the aftermath of a four-year war that had claimed the lives of more than eight thousand citizens. Many more returned home permanently wounded.[65] When so much suffering falls on a people with so much pride, a scapegoat must inevitably be found. And who caused white Mississippi so much suffering? The Union army. And yet, the secessionist government of Mississippi had just been soundly defeated by Federal troops. A second uprising was out of the question. Why were there now Federal troops stationed so visibly throughout the state? It was their duty to protect the recently freed slaves. And so, white Mississippi found its scapegoat. The conquered and disillusioned now had an outlet.

Another emotion would come to dominate a large portion of secessionist Mississippi: wrath.

IN THE AFTERMATH OF defeat, many whites took comfort in the racial ideology that told them that at least they weren't Black. Though defeated, they were still genetically superior to half the state. And they meant to assert and maintain that superiority.

After Reconstruction was effectively ended in 1877—an experiment that began with so much promise and was beginning to make political progress at the state level only to end in northern acquiescence to southern demands

Rolls of cotton in a field near Avalon in Carroll County, Mississippi. By Carol Highsmith (2016). *Library of Congress.*

(leading many to question why the Civil War was even fought)—white "Redeemers" retook the reins of government, and the disenfranchisement of Black citizens began in earnest. Lynching became a highly effective tool that kept Black people from the polls and the courthouses.

Carrollton, Mississippi
February 12, 1886

Ed and Charley Brown, two half-Choctaw, half-Black brothers, pulled up to the local Carrollton saloon to deliver their molasses. During the delivery, they bumped into Robert Moore, a white man from Greenwood, spilling molasses on his suit. An angry argument ensued but was quickly defused, and both sides concluded their business. It seemed as if the matter had been settled.

Weeks later, Moore was visiting with his friend James Monroe Liddell of Greenwood, and he told him of the confrontation in the saloon. Liddell, incensed that two Black men dared talk back to and argue with his white friend, promised revenge.

The next time Liddell saw the Brown brothers in town, on February 12, he accosted them, accusing them of both disrespecting his friend and not knowing their place. When the brothers argued back with Liddell, the latter flew into a rage and attempted to give the brothers a thrashing right there. Fortunately for all involved, Liddell was restrained by onlookers. Once again, the situation ended short of bloodshed. It was not defused—only reduced to a simmer.

Liddell walked down the street, entered the hotel and ordered dinner. As he ate and stewed over the brothers, word came to him that Ed and Charley were making threats of their own. Worse, for a white man in the era of the "Redeemers," the Black men were making disparaging remarks. Liddell, nearly choking with rage, leaped from his table and charged across the street, determined to make the two men pay for their insolence. This time, the confrontation would not be defused. Liddell slapped Ed in the face, and then the trio and their supporters drew guns.[66] Both parties began emptying their pistols at the other. In the end, both Liddell and the Brown brothers were wounded—Liddell in the elbow and thigh, Ed in the stomach and Charley in the shoulder.[67] Miraculously, all survived.

Word of the shootout quickly spread through Carrollton. Everyone with sense understood that the issue had not been settled. Repercussions would follow. But those repercussions were between the Browns and Liddell. Fights were the norm, and sometimes they ended in stabbings and shootings. Liddell would get his revenge, one way or another. No need to involve the law.

On March 12, the unfathomable happened. Ed and Charley Brown walked into the Carrollton County Courthouse and filed charges against James Liddell. Two men with Black blood in their veins had dared press criminal charges against a man who might have been their master only two decades before.

But the Fourteenth Amendment gave the brothers their rights as citizens—including the right to be heard by a fair and impartial legal system. The court date was set for March 17, 1886.

THIS WAS AN EARTHQUAKE, sending shockwaves throughout the surrounding region. Disbelief, shock and wrath permeated from the Carrollton County Courthouse, which had now become the epicenter of yet another war to preserve the "southern way." Black folks talking back to—and sometimes fighting with—whites happened on occasion. But a Black man taking a white man to court? On an equal footing? If the trial went forward, the entire Black community might see the courts as a viable option. And if the courts and legal system provided justice, the 1877 redemption had been for nothing.

No, the Brown brothers must be taught a lesson.

Carrollton County Jail
February 19, 1886

A vigilante mob appeared with the intent to send a message to the Black community, especially to Ed and Charley Brown. Their target was William McKinney, a nineteen-year-old Black man who had been convicted of manslaughter the previous October. Unfortunately for McKinney, his victim had been white. However, the local jury and judge must have sympathized with McKinney because he was given only a one-year sentence. He had seven more months to serve when the mob showed up around one in the morning on February 19, 1886.[68] The *New York Times* reported the events of that tragic night:

"KKK" by Adolfo Mexiac (1927). *New York Public Library.*

[T]hey seized a negro boy who had been committed to jail for having killed a white boy, but who had made out a good case of self-defense, and took him out of prison. They placed the rope intended for the negro man around the boy's neck, and without further ado hanged him to the limb of a tree.[69]

The local Carrollton paper was more detailed. McKinney was taken from the jail around one o'clock in the morning and marched down Lexington Street by twenty-five to fifty men with darkened faces. They placed a hangman's noose around his neck, and when McKinney began to scream, they rushed him to the horse rack and began to raise him. In their haste, they left his hands untied. Dangling in the air, McKinney raised himself onto the rack. Eager to kill the prisoner quickly, the mob opened fire, riddling the young man with forty to fifty bullets.[70]

The grand jury refused to indict anyone for the murder of William McKinney, although the jury did note, "We feel it our duty to condemn without reservation the act of barbarism visiting such terrible vengeance upon a helpless convict."[71]

The community's sympathy was little comfort to William McKinney.

THE LYNCHING OF McKINNEY was more than a threat. Nevertheless, the Brown brothers refused to retract their charges. Instead, they showed up as scheduled at the Carrollton County Courthouse on March 17, 1886. Ominously, Sheriff T.T. Hamilton was not present. James Liddell was, along with his lawyers and brother. More than two dozen Black men filled out their half of the courtroom.

Outside the ground rumbled under the hooves of sixty horsemen. Then, silence.

Anyone looking out one of the second-story windows would have immediately seen danger.

Heavy and fast-moving boots pounded up the staircase. One last moment of silence.

And then the doors were flung open and the massacre commenced. Roughly two-thirds of the attendees were Black. Of the twenty-three who were killed that afternoon, all were Black. Most, including Ed and Charley Brown, were killed upstairs. Some leaped out the window and were gunned down on the courthouse grounds. Only a few escaped.[72]

"ONE VOTE LESS."—*Richmond Whig.*

"One Vote Less" (1868). *Library of Congress.*

The mob had sent a clear and frightening warning to the Black community: the Federal troops were gone; the law now belonged to the Redeemers—and only to the Redeemers.

One week later, Jackson's *Clarion-Ledger* wrote of the massacre:

> *Do the people of Mississippi realize that at the door of the court-room in Carrollton in Carroll County the bloody bodies of its slain citizens lie heaped one upon another? They have not been removed. They cannot be removed. They will stay as a monument to the folly and the wickedness of their ruthless slayers.*

There can be no adequate punishment for the injury which has been inflicted upon the good people of Mississippi, by the murderous mob at Carrollton. There will be no punishment of any kind. Time spent in an attempt to bring them before the bar of that temple whose sanctity they have so grossly violated would be time thrown away.[73]

The *Clarion-Ledger* had issued a self-fulfilling prophecy. Not one member of the Carrollton mob was ever brought to justice.

Chapter 8

DEATH ON THE SABBATH

The Saga of Tom Garner

McComb
1898

Scott Causey sat in his living room, rocking in his chair, reading the Sunday paper. From the kitchen, he could perhaps hear the sounds of his wife preparing lunch: the chop of a knife on the block, corn husks being ripped off ears, potatoes boiling in a pot. It was quiet out in the country, with brush shielding the house from the road, acres of cropland growing in the back and copses of scrub oak breaking up the horizon. The paper rustled as Causey read.

He did not see the two steel barrels pointing toward him through his front window. He did not know that his last moments were at hand. An assassin had found him, and he aimed to kill him.

The shotgun exploded, and buckshot tore through Scott Causey's side. He was a big man, but the shot killed him almost instantly. He slumped over, thudding onto the floor, still gripping his newspaper.[74]

His wife, Maggie, was alarmed by the gunshot blast. Their house was small, and she must have rushed to the living room upon hearing the shot, must have seen her husband. She shot out of her back door in a panic.

Three hundred yards away, a neighbor lying in bed heard the gunshot. He sat up and looked toward the Causey home. He couldn't see the house—only a section of their yard. He was not too far away to make out a woman's scream: "Oh Lordy!"

Maggie Causey ran along her house, rounding the back corner. If she could make it to the public road in front, she might be able to find help. It was midmorning on a Sunday, and neighbors were bound to be traveling down the road on their way to Pisgah Church.

"Oh Lordy!" she screamed again.

She made it to the front yard. Now if she could just reach the gate and step into the road. But the assassin had no intention of allowing that. Anticipating her path, he moved to the yard. He stood between Maggie Causey and the front gate. As Maggie Causey approached, the assassin raised his shotgun with the coldness of a hunter marking a dove. Maggie Causey raised her arms. The assassin squeezed the trigger, and the other barrel of his shotgun spit fire.

Buckshot pierced Maggie Causey's body, ripping away her arm. She screamed once more, with the last of her vitality: "Oh Lordy!" And then she fell to the grass. She did not get up.

The assassin broke his shotgun, took two more shells from a pocket and reloaded. Then he walked to the raised foundation of the house, stooped and looked under. If there were any more Causeys around, he wanted to be sure to get them too. Not finding anyone, the assassin climbed onto the wide porch of the house and entered the front door.

From thirty-five feet away, two men watched from horseback. They were Buck Boggs and his son, John. They had been riding by the Causeys' house on their way to Pisgah Church as the first shotgun crack sounded out. Knowing that something was amiss, they wheeled their horses toward the Causey home, arriving just in time to see the assassin raise his shotgun for the second time.

"Stop," Buck Boggs said to his son. "He is going to shoot again." They watched as the assassin shot her down from point-blank range. They watched as he reloaded, checked under the house and disappeared. They sat there on their horses for a few minutes, stunned, discussing what to do next. Then they rode off, father toward the neighbor's house and son toward McComb.

They were eyewitnesses to the crime that papers would call "the most atrocious ever committed in this county." And their words would be crucial in catching, indicting and convicting the man who had ended the Causeys' lives that Sunday morning.

As Buck Boggs rode to spread the news of the murder, a thought repeated itself in his mind: *The baldheaded slink ought to be hanged before night.*[75]

Tom Garner. *Josh Foreman.*

TOM GARNER STRODE THROUGH the half mile of sandy farmland that separated his house from the Causeys'. He had one chance at beating a murder charge: he needed to get to Pisgah Church as fast as possible. If the entire community saw him at church, he'd have his alibi.

The Causeys should not have meddled in my daughter's relationship, he thought. *I warned them.*

Garner, carrying his double-barreled shotgun, stepped beside the cane patch, then between cotton and corn patches and finally through a watermelon patch. His shoes left imprints in the soil along the way—something he'd have to explain later. It took a few minutes to cover the distance between the two houses.[76]

He entered his own home and set his shotgun in a closet. He walked past his elder daughter, into the kitchen, where his wife was. He spent a moment talking to his wife. Then he changed hats, jumped on his horse and rode away fast toward the church.[77] Garner's wife emerged from the kitchen, crying. Tom had killed Mr. and Mrs. Causey, she told her daughter.

As Tom Garner galloped toward Pisgah Church, the events of the last few months must have replayed in his mind. Garner's daughter Allie married Scott and Maggie's son, Fred. Fred and Allie lived near the Causeys in a small house. The marriage had not gone well. There was talk of the two separating. Garner thought that Scott and Maggie *wanted* a separation, were *angling* for a separation.

Garner tried to tell Maggie Causey not to interfere. He had told her forcefully, standing in front of her house, not to interfere. "If you and Scott separate Fred and Allie, I'll kill both of you," he said. They were warned. John Carroll's wife heard the exchange. He wondered if she would tell anyone. *Of course she would.*

Other rumors circulated around McComb that did not point toward a harmonious relationship between the Garners and the Causeys. They said that Garner killed Scott Causey's dog. They said that Garner had threatened before to kill Scott Causey, threatened him while he was out in the woods working. He would deny it all, if it came to that. He would tell people that he was on good, neighborly terms with them. He would tell people that he had hauled Causey's crop to the gin the year before, ginned it and then hauled it back and spread it in the yard. When Causey had asked his price, he had refused payment. He was a good man.[78]

The morning of the murder, he was visiting his daughter. There was a disagreement about who owned what—his daughter or his son-in-law—inside the small house. He wanted his wife to accompany him back to the house, help settle it. But he decided instead to settle it with his shotgun. "I'll fix it," he told his wife before heading to the Causey home.

It took about an hour, normally, to reach Pisgah Church from Tom Garner's house. Riding hard, he would have made it there faster. He arrived sometime around 11:30 a.m. that morning. He hitched his horse and stood beside it for a few minutes. It was a prominent spot, where anyone arriving to church would notice him. J.S. Hayman saw him, as did Monroe Hayman, John H. Pine and Albert Creel.

Next Garner walked over to the well, a gathering spot where many men would stand and talk. He struck up a conversation with R.J. Wilson. Ves Thompson rode by and saw him there chatting. It was at the well that word of the double murder reached the church. It was about 11:45 a.m. Garner stood with a group as the news spread. He listened and must have reacted with shock, just like everyone else.

Inside, he must have been feeling panic. If word of the murder had spread that fast to the church, arriving just minutes behind him, then did someone witness it? Did someone see him there? If so, he could expect to be arrested at any moment. And yet no one seemed to suspect him of anything.

He proceeded to the church building and stepped "under the tabernacle," where he would be noticed by more congregants. *I just might get away with this….*

FRANK M. LEE WAS worshiping at his own church in McComb when word reached him that the Causeys had been murdered. As the marshal of McComb, he sprang into action, riding for the Causeys' house about a mile and a quarter west of town.[79] When he arrived, he found a dozen men gathered; the body of Maggie Causey was still lying in the yard.

Several men brought his attention to something suspicious. There were footprints in the soil, leading from the Causeys' house north toward Garner's. The tracks led through the Causeys' backyard, out to the cane patch and on to the fence that separated Garner's property from the Causeys'. It seemed that someone had climbed the fence recently, leaving dirt on a fence board and a track on the other side pointing toward Garner's. Lee suspected immediately that Tom Garner had committed the murders.

Noon at Delta Cotton Mills in McComb, Mississippi. By Lewis Wickes Hine (1911). *Library of Congress.*

He dispatched W.F. Conerly to Garner's house, telling him to confiscate his shotgun. When Conerly arrived, he found that Garner had not yet returned home from church. He asked Garner's wife for the shotgun, and Garner's daughter retrieved it and handed it to Conerly.

It had two barrels, had been recently fired and was loaded with two fresh shells. When Conerly checked the size of the load in the shells, he found that it was no. 6 shot—the same size as the shot that riddled the bodies of Scott and Maggie Causey.[80]

The footprints and the shotgun were enough evidence for Lee to act. He began riding west toward Pisgah Church. Tom Garner had spent his last day as a free man.

Lee met him on the road and told him that he was under arrest for the murders of Scott and Maggie Causey. Fearing that a mob would try to lynch Garner if he stayed in the area, Lee took Garner to the jail in Jackson.

Justice was swift in those days, and about two weeks after he was arrested, Garner was convicted of the murders and sentenced to hang.

But a twist of fate delayed his execution: Garner's lawyers appealed to the Mississippi Supreme Court. One of the jurors in the trial, they argued, was related by marriage to the victims. The Supreme Court agreed, overturning the conviction.

Garner would have to be tried again. He was, several months later, and this time was found innocent of the murder of Maggie Causey. At the center of the decision was the behavior of Buck Boggs and his son—the two eyewitnesses to the murder—on the day of the murder. They had ridden around the area telling people that Scott Causey had killed his wife. The "baldheaded slink" that Buck Boggs had seen was Scott Causey, but that was impossible—the Boggses did not realize that Scott Causey lay dead in his living room at the time his wife was murdered.

They later swore that they had seen Garner; apparently they told other people, "Mr. Causey had killed his wife" because Garner was at large and they feared that if they spread the word that Garner had done the murders, Garner would run.

The state had one more chance to prove that Garner had committed the murders. It would try him for Scott Causey's murder and hope for a conviction and a death sentence.

Ultimately, it was the testimony of Garner's own daughter that brought about a conviction. She had previously refused to share what she had seen and heard the morning of the murders. She did not want to incriminate her own father.

But her husband persuaded her to testify and share the story of how Tom Garner had stormed out of the house, shotgun in hand, promising to "fix it." How he had returned ten minutes later and told her mother what he had done before riding off to church.

In his third trial for murder, Garner was convicted of murder and sentenced to life in prison. He spent eleven years in state custody before being pardoned by acting governor Luther Manship in 1911.[81]

Chapter 9

ALEXANDER McCLUNG, THE BLACK KNIGHT OF MISSISSIPPI

Alexander McClung was the "hard-drinking homicidal miscreant" nephew of Supreme Court chief justice John Marshall. He was also one of the United States' most famous duelists. The red-haired, pipe-smoking son of Kentucky moved at a young age to a frontier where his courage, ruthlessness and marksmanship would be better appreciated: Mississippi.

McClung would also become one of the most colorful and deadliest characters in Mississippi history. He "behaved like a character out of Gothic fiction, dressing from time to time in a flowing cape, giving overripe oratory and morbid poetry, and terrifying many of his fellow Mississippians with his penchant for intimidation and violence."[82] McClung's wrathful courage would win him the admiration of some, the respect of many, the contempt of more and, in the end, a violent, lonely death.

South America
1827

As a navy enlistee, Alexander Keith McClung had spent more time fighting his fellow sailors than the enemy. No slight was too small for McClung to ignore, and he had a habit of exaggerating his grievances, often to the point of exchanging blows. After two years of brawling, McClung's temper finally—and inevitably—led to his first duel, at nineteen years old. He and his opponent met on a beach in South America. His shot tore off his opponent's thumb. McClung was hit in the arm as he tried to protect himself from the retaliatory shot. Not only was the young duelist seriously wounded, but he was also unemployed, forced to resign in order to avoid prosecution.[83] But the young man had found his passion and avocation: dueling.

Kentucky to Mississippi
1828

Stranded in Brazil after his resignation, McClung made his way back home to Kentucky. After fighting a duel with a relative (whom he killed), McClung promised his mother that he would control his temper and would never again issue a challenge. He then moved to Mississippi, where he bounced between Columbus, Jackson and Vicksburg. At the time, Mississippi was the Old Southwest and conveniently located along the Mississippi River—an ideal locale in which to settle disputes, violently.

At first, McClung was a fair to middling success. He had the skills to succeed as a lawyer. Historian H. Grady Howell claimed, "He had all the capability and all the theatrics and he certainly had friends, but he was evidently lazy and didn't want to do all the background work a lawyer has to do."[84]

Nevertheless, McClung established himself in his new home state and began to dabble in a variety of pastimes: poetry, law, journalism and politics. And dueling, of course.

Jackson, Near the Pearl River
1834

True to his promise to his mother, McClung never issued another challenge. But his volatile nature and unfiltered tongue provided ample opportunity for ritual killing. General Augustus Allen was McClung's next victim. Because he was challenged, McClung had the right to choose the weapons. He picked four pistols, two each, along with two Bowie knives. The two would

Digital illustration of Alexander Keith McClung, the "Black Knight of the South," based on a sketch that appeared in the *Hinds County Gazette* in 1923. *Josh Foreman.*

commence the duel at eighty paces, firing at will. If neither was incapacitated after the fourth shot, they would end the fight with their knives. Allen fired first and missed. McClung then shouted, "Are you content?" Allen was not. McClung then promised, "Then I'll hit you in the teeth!" At a little more than one hundred feet, McClung took aim and fired. The ball tore through General Allen's mouth, killing him within mere minutes. It was the longest kill shot in the history of U.S. duels.[85]

General Allen's death convinced the Mississippi legislature to outlaw duels.

December 29, 1838

McClung accepted the challenge of John Menifee, a congressman from Kentucky. The duel would take place across the river from Vicksburg at 11:00 a.m. and would be settled with rifles. Spectators began arriving at daybreak. By noon, between six and seven hundred people had arrived to watch the fight. Shortly after, and fashionably late, McClung arrived, at ease and cheerful. He promptly dropped his pistol and Bowie knife on the ground, took his rifle and approached his assigned spot. The two exchanged fire, with McClung's ball passing inches over Menifee's head and the latter's whizzing just by McClung's abdomen before lodging in a fence directly behind him.

The duel could have ended then. But that was not McClung's style. Instead, he hurled his gun down, screaming that his rifle had gone off before he had time to aim. (An eyewitness claimed that he had aimed exactly where the ball just missed—right by his adversary's head.)

McClung and Menifee retired to prepare for a second round. Fifteen minutes later, they were at their assigned spots. This time, Menifee did not get a chance to fire. McClung's ball slammed into Menifee's rifle. The remainder of the ball ricocheted into Menifee's head, just above his right eye.[86]

In the coming months, six of Menifee's relatives, attempting to avenge their kinsman, challenged McClung to a duel. All six died on the dueling field.[87]

Monterrey, Mexico
September 21–24, 1846

American troops were pinned down outside Monterrey. A deadly fire was raining down on them from a Mexican fort. Suddenly, troops from

Above: Storming of Palace
Hill at the Battle of
Monterey. By H.S. Sadd
(1855). *Library of Congress.*

Right: Jefferson Davis,
from *Confederate Generals
and Statesmen* by Charles
Magnus (circa 1863).
*Beinecke Library at Yale
University.*

JEFFERSON DAVIS

C. S. A.

Tennessee and Mississippi leaped up and stormed the works. Someone had ordered the charge. Exactly who would be hotly debated in the coming years. No one, however, doubted who was the first over the enemy walls: Lieutenant Colonel Alexander McClung. Within minutes, the Americans were in control of the fort.

But McClung was not satisfied. Having noticed enemy fire from a stone building to the rear of the fort, McClung charged again. This time, he was shot down, grievously wounded. The Mexicans counterattacked, and the battle raged around him. In the noise and confusion, McClung was left behind when the Americans withdrew. That evening, Colonel Jefferson Davis sent a contingent back to rescue McClung. Later, Davis would wish that he had not.

The irascible McClung had been shot through the hand, the bullet carrying bone fragments into his hip that later had to be surgically removed. Losing two fingers should have effectively ended his dueling career.[88] It did not.

Nor did merely being alive—and a national hero at that—alleviate his wrath. (In fact, being alive might have exacerbated his wrath, for as one newspaper account claimed, "Wearied of life, disappointed and [un] satisfied, he wooed the embraces of death. With hope of being slain, he enlisted in the Mexican War.")[89] Instead, he turned his venom on Jefferson Davis when the latter's star eclipsed his own after Davis's astonishing victory at Buena Vista. McClung would continue to hurl verbal taunts at the future Confederate president and would claim he regretted that Davis was one man he never got to kill in a duel.[90]

Bolivia
1850

On July 3, 1850, McClung was appointed by his former commander, President Zachary Taylor, the *charge d'-affaires* in Bolivia. His appointment lasted only one year. McClung was dismissed when he shot dead a British statesman for refusing to stand for "The Star-Spangled Banner."[91]

1851–55

McClung—disgraced statesman, failed lawyer and crippled duelist— grew increasingly isolated, as what few friends he had began distancing

Dueling pistols. By Simeon North (circa 1815–1820). *Metropolitan Museum of Art.*

themselves from the now embittered and unpopular has-been. McClung, always angry at the world, grew bitter toward his former companions and finally turned on himself. He drank more and more, often more than a gallon at a sitting, and supplemented his drinking with laudanum.[92] An observer noticed McClung in a local Jackson restaurant and noted the fall of the once esteemed war hero: "He had a large dueling pistol on either side of a bottle of wine that stood before him, and [a] bowie-knife was disposed between them. His face was deeply flushed and his bloodshot eyes gleamed angrily."[93]

Jackson
March 24, 1855

Alexander McClung checked into the Eagle Hotel in Jackson, Mississippi. He hired a carpenter to come to his room and carve the back of his chair into a "V" shape. The carpenter obediently altered the chair and left. McClung then bathed, combed his red hair and put on his finest outfit. He picked up a poem he had written and pinned it to his shirt. He sat on the chair and rested his head in the newly carved chair back. McClung then picked up his dueling pistol, the weapon that had ended so many lives, and

The Eagle and Bowman Hotels historical marker. *Joseph Starrett.*

placed it against his temple. He pulled the trigger, and his head fell back into the "V," leaving his clothes and final poem unscathed:[94]

"Invocation to Death"

Swiftly speed o'er the wastes of time,
Spirit of Death.
In manhood's morn, in youthful prime,
I woo thy breath.
For the glittering hues of hope are fled
Like the dolphin's light;
And dark are the clouds above my head
As the starless night.
Oh, vainly the mariner signs for the rest
Of the peaceful haven,
The pilgrim saint for the shrines of the blest,
The calm of heaven;
The galley slave for the night wind's breath,
At burning noon;
But more gladly I'd spring to thy arms, O Death,
Come soon, come soon![95]

McClung's corpse and poem were found exactly as he planned, exactly as he posed. His body was taken back to Vicksburg, the city where so many of his duels began, and buried at Cedar Hill Cemetery.

SLOTH

....

Despite their desires, the lazy will come to ruin, for their hands refuse to work.
—Proverbs 21:25

Bogged in this slime they say, "Sluggish we were
in the sweet air made happy by the sun,
and the smoke of sloth was smoldering in our hearts;
now we lie sluggish here in this black muck!"
This is the hymn they gurgle in their throats
but cannot sing in words that truly sound.
—Dante, Inferno *VIII, 121–26*

Chapter 10

MISSISSIPPI

The Silent Society

Money, Mississippi
August 28, 1955

Three men pulled up to Reverend Moses Wright's home in Money, Mississippi. They demanded to see the "fat boy from Chicago," the Black fourteen-year-old who, three days earlier, had whistled at a white woman. Forcing their way in at gunpoint, they dragged the teenager to their truck, where a woman identified him as the culprit. Placing their victim in the truck, the foursome drove off.

Elizabeth Wright frantically ran to her white neighbors begging for help. Her great-nephew had been kidnapped. She feared for his life. Her neighbors did nothing.

Terrified, Moses Wright drove around in the early hours of Sunday morning looking for the boy he had been entrusted with. Unable to find Emmett, he sent his own children to stay with neighbors, and he warned another boy he had promised to look after—who had been part of his son's and Emmett's party the day of the whistling incident—to move to another house and take the first train back to Chicago. Wright then notified the sheriff of the kidnapping. The lawman did nothing.

Three days later, Till's tortured body was found tied to a gin fan along the banks of the Tallahatchie River. Two half brothers—Roy Bryant and J.W. Milam—were indicted for murder.

Emmett Till and his mother, Mamie Till. *U.S. Department of the Interior.*

Four weeks after the grisly murder, twelve white men retired to determine the fate of Bryant and Milam. The half brothers' guilt had been established. The nation knew it and the state knew it, but most importantly, the local community knew it. (Not only did Bryant and Milam boast of their murder to *Look* magazine for a $4,000 payment shortly after their acquittal, but both men were also soon living out of state, having been ostracized by their own community, and were denied necessary loans from their bank.) The community knew their guilt. And still the jury acquitted the killers. The twelve jurors could have taken a stand against oppression, injustice and Jim Crow. They could have taken the most basic of all stands: against the murder of an innocent person. Yet they did nothing.[96]

Jackson, Mississippi
June 12, 1963

Medgar Evers picked up a box of T-shirts logoed "Jim Crow Must Go." He was exhausted after a less than fruitful meeting with fellow activists. He hadn't seen his wife and three children all day. Excited by President John F. Kennedy's televised promise earlier that night to sign into law civil rights legislation but tired of living with anxiety, fear and constant threats on his life, Evers was looking forward to a few hours' sleep before restarting his Sisyphean battle in the morning.

Medgar Evers. *Smithsonian National Museum of African American History and Culture.*

He never made it to his bed. He never made it to his front door. An assassin's bullet pierced his heart. He stood up and staggered across his carport toward his door. His wife, Myrlie, found him bleeding out and rushed him to the hospital, where he died within an hour.

Meanwhile, the assassin, Byron De La Beckwith, was driving back to his house in Greenwood. He was driving back without his rifle, which he had dropped in a panic in a honeysuckle thicket across the street from Evers's home when a neighbor came out firing his pistol in the air.

A frightened De La Beckwith soon recovered his nerves, proud of his accomplishment and confident that the citizens of Jackson would maintain the same wall of silence that had protected Roy Bryant and J.W. Milam. De La Beckwith's confidence was justified. Two trials in the immediate aftermath of the murder ended in hung juries.

Once again, a preferential option for silence suppressed justice.[97]

Neshoba County, Mississippi
June 21, 1964

James Chaney, Andrew Goodman and Michael Schwerner sat in the Philadelphia, Mississippi jail. They had been arrested for speeding. They would soon be murdered for being Jewish and Black.

Goodman and Schwerner had joined Chaney in Mississippi during Freedom Summer to help register Black citizens to vote. While the three sat in prison, the deputy sheriff informed the Ku Klux Klan that the racial agitators would soon be released. They were. And then they were abducted again. It would be the last time the three were seen alive.

It became apparent that something was dreadfully amiss when the activists failed to check in with their parent organization. A day passed with no word of the trio's whereabouts. And then another day. And another. Soon everyone realized that the civil rights workers would not be coming back. It was now only a matter of locating the bodies.

And then the cordon of silence encircled another Mississippi community. Even with the eyes of the nation on Neshoba County, and the Federal

Bureau of Investigation and U.S. Navy searching for the missing men, the community remained silent. Nothing turned up. The pressure mounted, but still silence. By the end of July, more than one thousand Mississippians had been questioned by the FBI (including five hundred known Klansmen) and still nothing.[98]

Finally, after six weeks, the FBI received a tip: the three men were buried in a dam on private land outside Philadelphia.[99]

Three nights later, on August 7, a memorial service was held in Meridian for James Chaney. White Methodist minister Ed King stepped to the forefront and delivered the following eulogy, summed up by Charles Marsh:

> [Who killed James Chaney?] *Not just the vicious klansmen who carried out the assassination. James Chaney's blood lies on the hands of the FBI and the United States government, on complacent Americans from all parts of the country, but especially on the silent white Christians of the state. These people are just as guilty as the "sick white Mississippians" who carried out the brutal murder, "and more damned in their souls because they know it's wrong. The greatest tragedy that has occurred here is not just these deaths but the failure in the white community that has brought this about, that has tolerated it."*
>
> "The white Christians of the city of Meridian, tonight, need your prayers because God almighty sees them and knows in his eyes that every white Christian that did not come to this church is no Christian." *Every white Christian who did not come to this church is guilty, not only of violence and cruelty, but of forsaking and betraying the call of Christ.*
>
> *Look! The symbol of white Mississippi has become a burning cross. What more graphic expression of its own death could be imagined?*[100]

Ed King's clarion call to stand up for basic human rights was heeded by some. But not enough.

Jackson, Mississippi
November 23, 1967

A thunderclap exploded across the neighborhood. The sound of fallen wood and shattered glass followed. Stunned and scared neighbors stepped outside, and all eyes were drawn to the smoldering house of civil rights activist

Rabbi Perry Nussbaum. The rabbi's wife, Arene, was in the yard sobbing and picking glass out of her hair and clothes. Rabbi Nussbaum yelled at a neighbor to call his friend, Pastor Douglas Hudgins of Jackson's First Baptist Church, and plead with him to use his position to condemn this senseless violence from the pulpit.

The next morning, the rabbi, pastor, president of the Jackson Rotary Club and Governor Paul Johnson stood together surveying the damaged house. Only two months before, Nussbaum's synagogue had also been bombed. Being a Jew had once again become a de facto crime, if not de jure.

The angry rabbi then turned to Mississippi's most respected and prominent minister: "If you had spoken out from your pulpit after the synagogue was bombed and told your people it was wrong to have done that, this wouldn't have happened!" As Hudgins tried to offer his condolences, Nussbaum interrupted: "Don't tell me how sorry you are. Those sons-of-a-gun attacked me and my family! They've attacked my house! I don't want to hear how sorry you are! Doug, if you're really sorry about this, get on the pulpit Sunday and tell your people this is wrong. Talk to those segregationists that fill up your church."

The next Sunday, Rabbi Nussbaum sat next to his radio and listened to Hudgins's sermon at First Baptist. Without mentioning Nussbaum, Hudgins proceeded to tell his people that it is wrong to bomb houses. No mention of antisemitism. No mention of desegregation. No mention of civil rights.[101] Instead, Hudgins turned his attention to what Minister Ed King calls "disidentification." "Respectable whites" attributed violent and racist attacks to a fringe group of fanatics. These fanatics were "so far outside the circle (and class) of the religious moderates that there was still no need to accept any responsibility for their (the Klan, the red necks, the poor whites, the hill billies, the white trash, etc.) violent acts."[102]

Most white Mississippians turned their religion "otherworldly" and shunned the Social Gospel, becoming in the process what Father Bill Henry calls the "Frozen Chosen."[103] Even Nussbaum's own congregation tried to curtail his civil rights activism and simply accept the status quo.[104] Ole Miss professor James Silver's proclamation three years earlier was once again confirmed: "In the past year or two, many individual preachers and a few ministerial groups have made courageous stands, but the church as a whole has placed its banner with the status quo."[105]

EVEN CASUAL HISTORIANS KNOW of Roy Bryant, J.W. Milam, Byron De La Beckwith, Edgar Ray Killen and the Ku Klux Klan. These men and the evil they represented are remembered in infamy. But there is another segment of humanity that enabled the heinous to occur: the Silent Ones.

The Silent Ones fell into several categories: the frightened, the silenced and the uncomfortable. Many Mississippians were too frightened to speak up. The Ku Klux Klan dominated the imagination of Mississippians—white and Black—throughout the 1950s and '60s. The cross burnings, beatings and lynching of Black persons are well documented, but white persons in the state experienced similar reprisals. One need look no further than the murders of Goodman and Schwerner in Philadelphia. Whites, too, lived in perpetual fear of the Klan and of the consequences of taking a countercultural stand.

Even federal marshals and jury members were threatened in the build-up, during and after a trial with racial overtones. At one such trial, a defendant promised: "We've got dynamite for them if they find us guilty." Two jury members awoke to burning crosses in their yards. A jury foreman, Langdon Anderson, received a phone call letting him know, "It's important that certain things be done." Anderson's son recalls, "For a long time after the trial, my dad always checked under the hood to make sure nothing was planted there."[106] FBI inspector Joseph Sullivan claimed, "They [the KKK] owned the place. In spirit everyone belonged to the Klan."[107] But what Sullivan failed to realize was that most White Mississippians did not belong to the Klan "in spirit." Instead, their spirit had been killed by the Klan. Fear of economic reprisals, fear of social ostracism, fear of a firebomb in the middle of the night and fear of death silenced many good-hearted Mississippians. Fear caused Mississippi to become what Bill Minor described as "the KGB of the cotton patches."[108] Or, as Charles Marsh claimed, "If you were a Klan militant searching the night for the civil rights heretics, you would count it fortunate that the pure souls had turned their sight inward."[109]

A far bolder, but significantly smaller segment of the population was made up of those who did fight back against Jim Crow. Most of these were censored. Many were sent to prison. Some were murdered. Those with the courage to speak often had no outlet, no platform. Most papers served the status quo. The television stations cooperated with the establishment. The church pulpits promoted patience and accommodation. Douglas Hudgins was not alone in his aversion to meddling in secular affairs. Civil rights historian John Dittmer claimed, "Mississippi had no racially enlightened white political leadership, no locally influential voices of moderation in the media, no white ministerial associations pleading for racial justice."[110]

Even the Catholic Church, with its more liberal attitude toward integration and civil rights, often sat on the sidelines, unwilling to rock the proverbial boat. SNCC project leader Mary Lane recalls the silence of the Greenwood Catholic Church:

> *I remember when SNCC first came into Greenwood, the* [current] *leaders of the* [Greenwood] *Movement wouldn't have anything to do with SNCC, you know. And this sort of thing hurts.... They* [the Catholics] *still have a paper, the* Centerlight. *You know, we went to them and we pleaded with them to print something about SNCC in the paper. And they refused to do it.*[111]

James Silver quoted an Ole Miss professor at the time: "Men of good will who are content to sit on their hands silently hoping that nothing will rock the boat are seemingly unaware that the use of their oars might stay the foundering craft; these men are not leaders, nor are they followers."[112] And those who were willing to take a stand, to pick up an oar, often found themselves without an outlet, without a pulpit, without a voice.

A third segment of Mississippians were described by Rabbi Charles Mantinband in May 1962: "Life can be very placid and gracious in this part of the country—if one runs with the herd. The South is turbulent

Fannie Lou Hamer at the Democratic National Convention in 1964. *Library of Congress.*

and sullen and sometimes noisy, but there is a conspiracy of silence in respectable middle-class society. Sensitive souls, with vision and the courage of the Hebrew prophets, are drowned out. Timid souls, complacent and indifferent, seldom articulate their protests."[113] In short, the beatings, the burnings and the lynchings made many Mississippians uncomfortable. Injustice, ugliness and evil anywhere makes good-hearted people cringe. Combined with the siege mentality of many Mississippians who perceived their state to be under constant scrutiny and criticism from outsiders—some justified, much not—it caused the average person to look the other way.

Despite the silence of most Mississippians, civil rights activist Fannie Lou Hamer saw hope for the future, even amid the darkness of the 1960s. Using the analogy of one of Jesus's most famous parables, she pointed out that her home state was full of Levites and priests, but there were Good Samaritans as well:

> *Although they were strangers, they were the best friends we ever met. This was the beginning of the New Kingdom in Mississippi. To me, if I had to choose today between the church and these young people—and I was brought up in the church and I'm not against the church—I'd choose these young people. They did something in Mississippi that gave us the hope that we had prayed for so many years. We had wondered if there was anybody human enough to see us as human beings instead of animals. These young people were so Christlike.*[114]

Regrettably, Hamer was referring mostly to the out-of-state activists who flocked to Mississippi in the 1960s to help their Black brethren. It took an army of outsiders to mobilize the local silent ones.

Chapter 11

THE CAT BAPTIST

Kiah Lincecum Finds His Place

Kiah Lincecum materialized on the Georgia frontier just before the Revolution. Born to conflict, he would grow into a cracker, a lazy lubber, a ragged squatter, an eye-gouger, a white savage—all names historian Nancy Isenberg might ascribe to him, in addition to "white trash." He would become an "unwholesome type" who "lived a brute existence in a dingy log cabin, with yelping dogs at his heels, a haggard wife, and a mongrel brood of brown and yellow brats to complete the story." Multiple log cabins—and multiple wives, actually. He would become a Mississippian.[115]

Kiah's father was an Indian fighter at a time when the southern frontier was contested, in the late 1770s. He led a gang of one hundred rangers up and down the Oconee River, their goal to do violence against the resident Creeks.

The strip of land between the Oconee and Ogeechee Rivers was a defensive front for the tribe, a boundary line stretching from the north to the south, stopping further white encroachment into Indian country. The land had been ceded to the United States by Cherokees, but the Creeks claimed the land as well and were furious that whites were trying to annex it. The Creeks raided settlers in that strip of land more than 1,100 times from 1770 to 1799, stealing hundreds of horses and killing more than two hundred settlers.[116]

One of those settlers was Kiah's father; he was ambushed, killed and scalped five times. A scalp *can* be removed in strips.

His mother fled Georgia, taking her six children—Kiah the youngest— east to the Edgefield District of South Carolina. When she returned to her

Georgia homestead seven years later, after peace had been declared between Britain and America, all she found was ash, ruins and "piles of charred wheat and rye where the barn had stood."[117]

As Kiah Lincecum's mother tried to rebuild her life in Georgia, a revenant of the Revolution wandered into her neighborhood. His name was Thomas Roberts, and he was a British deserter who had fought for the United States for the final three years of the war. The war between Britain and America had ended, but the border conflict between settlers and Creek had not abated; the Creek wanted the settlers gone, and the settlers were determined to keep their Georgia claims. Roberts parlayed his experience as a soldier into a career as an Indian fighter, and he enlisted Kiah, then about seventeen, to join his gang.

Kiah spent three years fighting alongside Roberts and returned a man—a big, strong, heavy-drinking man "fully able to whip every man in the settlement who dared oppose him."[118]

Kiah's youth had been fear, conflict, loss, displacement, impoverishment and more conflict. He was a settler who had lived a most unsettled life. The end of his term of enlistment with Roberts brought him back to his mother's home. His five siblings had grown up and moved out.

Shortly after, a traveling preacher paid the Lincecum household a visit. The preacher, Abram Brantley, was spreading a countercultural message—settlers on the American frontier need no longer obey the strictures of Anglicanism. They could put aside the Book of Common Prayer and embrace a more egalitarian and emotional form of worship: they could become Baptists. But if they accepted, their new faith would demand of them stricter self-discipline and the judgment of their church peers.[119]

The preacher asked Kiah and his mother to sing with him. When Kiah opened his mouth, his "firm, manly, melodious voice fairly made the heavenly arches ring." Kiah had a gift. With his strong body, handsome looks and angelic voice, the preacher told him, Kiah could become a great preacher of the gospel. "Lose no time," the preacher said. "Go to work."

Kiah embraced his new trajectory as a holy man. He told his church community of his sins, his rough upbringing. And they welcomed him, "not only as a worthy member, but as a bright star and ornament in the Church of God." Kiah was baptized and rose from the water "shouting praises and exhorting the people to flee from the wrath to come."

Kiah began attending Baptist meetings, preaching, and closing them out with his singing. The other congregants envisioned his future. *He will be a preacher, and a big one at that!*

"A Western Frontiersman" (1848). *Beinecke Library at Yale University.*

Kiah's preaching drew attention from a young woman, Sally Strange. Before long they were married—a preacher and a husband in such short order.

The act of baptism by immersion was central to the Baptist faith that was spreading across the southern frontier in the 1700s. Baptists believed that a person must choose to embrace salvation, to leave behind the "old, wrong, sinful" self and emerge a "new, right, forgiven" self. The act of submersion in water was the symbolic turning point that marked a new commitment to Christian faith.[120]

The Baptists placed enormous importance on the act of baptism. So it was understandable that Kiah Lincecum's peers were aghast when the loud, enthusiastic man grabbed a wayward feline by the fur and dipped it beside the river. "In the name of the father, and the son, and the holy spirit," he might have said, "I baptize you, Mr. Scratchy," the cat twisting, scratching, biting, mewling, kicking up river water, trying to escape from Kiah's grip.

Word of the blasphemy spread fast. Two hundred years later, a descendant of Kiah's would dig into church records and discover that he had threatened to rape a woman—no mention of the cat baptism was included in the record. Discussions were had, a vote was taken and Kiah was expelled from his church as swiftly as he had been embraced. His marriage ended.[121]

Kiah's career as a religious leader and as a husband had been cut short. But he was not the kind of man to let a setback set him back. He pivoted from religious education to general education. Although he was a man in his twenties, he enrolled at his settlement's log cabin school. There he met another Sally—Sally Hickman. She was only fourteen, but Kiah wanted her. They were married.

Kiah, remarried, abandoned his scholarly pursuits and set about making a living for himself and his soon-to-be pregnant wife. He collected a few possessions—a horse, a cow, a few hogs, a bed and some other furniture. At sixteen, Sally Lincecum gave birth to a large baby boy: Gideon. Kiah had become a father, but his wanderlust nagged. He found himself looking south to the Oconee River, where he had fought the Creeks as a boy.

Opportunity is there, he thought. *I can take it.*

It was around 1795. America had thrown off its British yoke, and Americans were looking south and west. Kiah looked south and west. He had been formed and primed. Now it was time for his charge to ignite. He set off, although he did not know it, for Mississippi. His odyssey is recounted here in succinct episodes.

MOVE NO. 1: WARREN COUNTY, GEORGIA, TO SCULL SHOALS, GEORGIA

Two years living in fear of the Creeks.

MOVE NO. 2: SCULL SHOALS TO WARREN COUNTY

Back to the safety of Warren County. A home near where Kiah had grown up. Kiah is the first to try growing cotton here. For three years, he raises it, picking out seeds with his fingers. He stuffs the cotton into meal sacks and hauls them to market, where they bring fifty cents per pound in silver. There is money in cotton! Would it grow better in Tennessee?

MOVE NO. 3: WARREN COUNTY, GEORGIA, TO SOMEWHERE IN GEORGIA

Kiah steers his team of four horses along the country road toward Tennessee. In his wagon, he carries a large chest, four beds, seven children (three white and four Black) and his eighty-eight-year-old mother. Kiah's mother begins to shake violently. The fits startle Kiah so much that he cuts the trip short. Near their camp, an old man named Morris has a house. Kiah asks if his mother can recuperate there. The old man agrees. Three weeks pass. Kiah wonders, "Can we just rent your place for a while?"
    A year of growing cotton and corn. Off, again, to Tennessee.

MOVE NO. 4: SOMEWHERE IN GEORGIA TO ABBEVILLE DISTRICT, SOUTH CAROLINA

Kiah's son Gideon walks beside the wagon, shooting at every bird he can see. In four days, they reach the Savannah River. Camp in the woods. Camp, by chance, with an old, drunk Irishman. Kiah and the Irishman disappear for three days. Kiah's family is alarmed. When he reemerges, he says, "Damn Tennessee—there is good land in South Carolina."
    Another year farming. Another urge to leave. Another wagon trip.

MOVE NO. 5: ABBEVILLE DISTRICT, SOUTH CAROLINA, TO ATHENS, GEORGIA

Everyone works in the cotton fields. By Christmas, nearly five thousand pounds of uncleaned cotton have been taken to the gin. Hundreds of dollars are earned. On the road again, to Tennessee or bust.

Sometime around now, Gideon Lincecum, just a boy, joins his father at a frontier ironworks. Kiah slides his arms under the beam of a forge hammer. The hammer is usually lifted up by a waterwheel, by the power of a flowing river. Kiah's body tenses, and slowly the 596-pound hammer rises from its resting place. Lincecum is a force of nature too—a six-foot-tall, two-hundred-pound settler of the American frontier. Gideon gapes in wonder. He will never forget it.[122]

Move no. 6: Athens, Georgia, to Pendleton District, South Carolina

Gideon is twelve years old. He runs alongside the wagon and far ahead of it, shooting and killing many birds. He shoots into the rivers and streams, spearing many fish with an iron-tipped arrow.

Kiah rides on the wagon, sharing a bottle of whiskey with his driver. They drink so much that the driver falls, spooking the horses. The horses tear off, destroying the wagon and badly injuring Kiah's elderly mother.

Kiah looks at a grove of peach trees nearby. He decides to stay and farm at that very spot. He hauls peaches to a still and turns them to brandy. He sells brandy to other men like him, passing through the country. There is money in brandy!

Kiah's brother visits, trailing eight motherless children. "West—west," he says. On the road again.

Move no. 7: Pendleton District, South Carolina, to the wild woods of Georgia

The Creeks finally abandon their claims to the land west of the Oconee, and Kiah resolves to claim his share. The state is offering, by lottery, parcels of two hundred acres to settlers. Kiah is irritated that he is not even given the chance to try for the lottery. But he has already moved to the spot he wants.

He is forced to leave. He gives all the money he has, and three slaves, for a cabin in the wild woods. A dozen acres are planted.

War of 1812. The Creeks lose more land. Mississippi Territory grows, and there is more land for men like Kiah to take. Kiah wants his.

Move no. 8: The wild woods of Georgia to Ocmulgee River, Georgia

It takes years for whites to settle the Creek land. They do. Kiah is one of them, but he hates settlement. There are other whites all around him. Load the wagons, gather the family. Kiah, Sally, Gideon, a mess of children and then slaves. Big dogs. Guns. On the road, west, and this time no stopping for a good long while.

MOVE NO. 9: OCMULGEE RIVER, GEORGIA, TO TUSCALOOSA, ALABAMA

For six weeks, Kiah and his brood roll along rough trails, shooting every turkey, deer and pigeon they can. They even shoot pike, firing an iron-tipped arrow into river water. They have the time of their lives—they are hogs at the trough, and the trough is filled with delicacies. They eat as much as they can.

They cut down cane at an unsurveyed spot and make clapboard houses. They live on bear meat and venison until there is none left. They pay too much for frontier provisions. But flour is costly this deep into the wild woods.

Some Creeks pass through the area on their way to exile, west of the Mississippi. Kiah goes west too, riding through the woods where there is no road. He rides for seventy-five miles until he reaches Mississippi, although no one knew of that political division yet. He stops at the Tombigbee River, somewhere near where Columbus, Mississippi, would grow up. *This is better,* he thinks. *There is no one here. No one but me.* He returns to Tuscaloosa and tells his son, "Time to go west again."

MOVE NO. 10: TUSCALOOSA, ALABAMA, TO MISSISSIPPI

For twelve days, Kiah and his brood hack a path through the woods. The women gather hickory nuts, chestnuts, muscadines and persimmons. There's so much they can barely get it all back to camp. The men shoot as many deer, turkeys, ducks and pigeons as they can. They sleep at night, and the howls of red wolves go up around them.

They reach the Tombigbee, and each chooses a spot along the river. Kiah Lincecum fulfills his destiny—he has finally become a Mississippian.[123]

WITHIN TWO DECADES, THE Choctaws and Chickasaws, who lived across the river from Kiah, would be forced west along the Trail of Tears.

Kiah Lincecum embodied all the seven deadly sins. He was slothful—he knew the value of farm work but opted as often as he could for life on the road chasing game and adventures. He was envious, always looking for better land, and greedy, always taking more. He was prideful to think that he

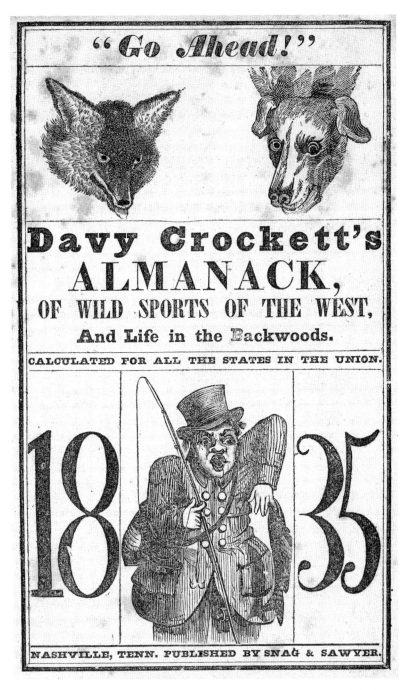

"Go Ahead!" From *Davy Crockett's Almanac of Wild Sports of the West and Life in the Backwoods* (1835). *Beinecke Library at Yale University.*

could become a preacher on a whim and, if his reputation as a brawler is an indication, wrathful. He was a glutton for alcohol and lustful, as his threat of rape showed.

But as flawed as he was, we may find that, just a little, we sympathize with Kiah and his quest to realize his own dream. He was a Mississippi maniac and an early father of our state. He is our cautionary tale and our instruction:

> Do Not don buckskin and a wide-brimmed hat, pack a horse with rifle and jug and look out desirous at the horizon...
> But...if you do...you may come alive out among the oaks.

Chapter 12

DAVE'S DARK HORSE TAVERN

Josh Foreman and Ryan Starrett

The present authors are under contract to write a book on the seven deadly sins in Mississippi history, with each sin being represented by three chapters.

Just before submission, we stand at twenty chapters. The one chapter we missed? It's likely the sin we're most guilty of.[124] Despite possessing PhDs in

Josh Foreman and Ryan Starrett at Dave's Dark Horse Tavern in Starkville, Mississippi. *Rachel Foreman.*

the seven deadly sins,[125] sloth would seemingly be at the bottom of our list of transgressions. We both work multiple jobs, pay our debts, pay our own ways and raise five children between our two families. *The gentleman doth protest too much, methinks*.

But a sin is not always a wicked act. It can be an omission, a failure to do good. Given the advantages of our birth, could we have done more? Could we be more? How many opportunities have we squandered?

Hopefully the above procrastinatory soliloquy will satisfy our publisher's expectations of twenty-one chapters. We could write one, but there's the challenge of finding an applicable story, the editing, the revising, the editing, the revising, the feedback and more editing and revising. Reading and re-reading and re-re-reading....

So, to all our readers who were hoping for another story in this part, we're sorry, but we're going to go to Dave's Dark Horse Tavern to have a beer.

GREED

....

For in vain is a net spread
in the sight of any bird,
but these men lie in wait for their own blood;
they set an ambush for their own lives.
Such are the ways of everyone who is greedy for unjust gain;
it takes away the life of its possessors.
—Proverbs 1:17–19

For all the gold that is or ever was
Beneath the moon won't buy a moment's rest
For even one among these weary souls.
—Dante, Inferno *VII, 64–66*

Chapter 13

TOWHEAD WHITE
AND THE STATE LINE MOB

El Ray Hotel
Corinth, Mississippi
April 2, 1969

Another victim lay dead on the grounds of Corinth's El Ray Hotel. The victim lay back in the driver's seat of his car as if he had dozed off. Only his eyes were wide open. Pink puss was bubbling out of his forehead. Blood covered his face and chest. His left hand still clenched a .38-caliber pistol. A bloodied bag of silver quarters lay behind the driver's seat.[126]

Mississippi-Tennessee State Line
1950s

That night, the morgue received another body. Business picked up for the morticians of the Mississippi-Tennessee state line in the 1950s when the whorehouses, gambling dens and stills of Phenix City, Alabama, were shut down. The gangsters simply moved west.

Conveniently located on the highway between two states—where local rivalries over jurisdiction naturally arose—the state line provided the perfect setting for experienced and would-be criminals. While many of these felons were simple toughs, plenty were highly intelligent, persuasive, hardworking men and women who might have made an honest living and contributed to society. Instead, the lure of the fast buck and then, once acquired, the lure of more and more and more led to the swindle of countless, the imprisonment of some and the deaths of too many (or not enough, depending on your perspective).[127]

Mississippi-Tennessee State Line
1956

Carl Douglas "Towhead" White had finally found a home. The Mississippi-Tennessee line was the perfect place for an enterprising man like himself. He determined to make its environs—and the cash that flowed therein—his personal fiefdom.

Born in Sumner, Mississippi, the handsome, slender, smooth-talking six-foot-two criminal had put together an impressive rap sheet by the time he moved to the state line. An air force deserter at the age of fifteen, White promptly picked up another enlistment bonus when he joined the army one year later.[128] Four years later, he was in Parchman Prison after a failed robbery attempt in Vance, Mississippi, during which he was shot; he was transported to and escaped from a Memphis hospital and was finally captured in El Paso. After only one year in Mississippi's most notorious prison, he was back at the state line, determined to enrich himself on ill-begotten loot.

It did not take long for local law enforcement to realize that they had an unusually sharp con man operating on their turf, a turf already full of kindred spirits. Idolizing Al Capone, Towhead White was determined to become king of them all.[129]

And yet the state line was ruled by a queen. Louise Anderson arrived at the state line from West Point, Mississippi, in 1937. She soon married Jack Hathcock, an up-and-coming gangster who, within a dozen years, had built his own fiefdom along the state line. Although the border was full of pimps, gamblers and bootleggers, Jack soon became

Digital illustration of Towhead White, based on a photo of him that circulated after his murder. *Josh Foreman.*

the most notorious. But to Louise Hathcock, her husband had served his purpose, and she began to gradually take over his operation, from managing the books to running the scams to eliminating potential threats—by bribes, beatings and sometimes murder.

It did not take Louise long to fall for Towhead White. It took Towhead even less time to recognize a cash cow. The aging and fading beauty became more attractive as her operation expanded and bank account grew.

Shamrock Motel
McNairy County, Tennessee
May 22, 1964

Louise Hathcock sent a runner across the state line to summon her husband to her room at the Shamrock Motel. Towhead White waited until she entered her room and then pounced on top of her, beating her sides and arms as her screams were muffled by a pillow.

A drunk Jack Hathcock stumbled across from his nightclub, the White Iris, just across Highway 45. He knocked and entered to find his wife in a blue negligee and then stared, confused, at her battered body. At that moment, Towhead stepped from the corner and fired three bullets into the cuckolded husband. Surprisingly, Jack Hathcock still had life enough to stumble out of the motel room and back toward his club before bleeding out. Jack Hathcock was buried the next day in Corinth, Mississippi.

Louise Hathcock showed the sheriff and judges her bruises that she claimed came from her husband, and the murder charges were dismissed. Towhead White had already made plans to fleece Louise of her recent inheritance.[130]

Three vignettes illustrate the lengths to which Towhead White would go to make a dollar. His scams and heists continued throughout his life. The bail he posted, the time he served in prison and the possibility of being killed makes one wonder if his greed incapacitated his reason.

St. Louis, Missouri
1961

Towhead White was working on the safe in a large St. Louis department store. Only the safe's door stood between him and more than $26,000. And that door was cracking fast. Then Towhead's partner from New Orleans ran up, warning that the night watchman was closing in. Surprised and then angry at the setup man for not forewarning him about a guard, the two hid behind some boxes, hoping that the watchman walked on by. He didn't. He noticed that the safe had been tampered with and whipped out his pistol. Towhead pounced on him and beat the guard into unconsciousness.

After tipping the negligent setup man, Towhead headed back to Corinth with his share of the loot—$8,673.[131]

Biloxi, Mississippi
March 25, 1965

Towhead sat at a blackjack table in the casino at the Red Carpet. Three men armed with tommy guns entered the hotel and promptly collected $11,500 from the manager and safe, lining up the anxious customers against a wall. Towhead sat unmolested at his table. Hours later, he was arrested at the same blackjack table, gambling as if he had expected the robbery. He had—he planned it.[132]

Alabama
1966–68

Towhead drove his Cadillac across the state line—only this time it was the Alabama state line. He planned to meet up with one of the Yellowhammer State's most notorious gangsters, Dewitt Dawson, a man in and out of prison for "murder, drugs, robberies, and bootlegging."[133] The gangster duo was a match made in hell, as they quickly began binging on bootleg liquor, bedding the willing (and often; taking into account their personal charm and good looks, they had their choice) and beating up anyone questioning their moral code.

Towhead and Dewitt's most profitable venture was robbing high-stakes poker games. Dewitt, knowing well the gamblers of the region, would sit playing at a poker table that required large antes and larger buy-ins. After relieving himself in the restroom, he would unlock a back door on his way to the table. Moments later, an armed Towhead burst in and collected both money and attire from the players before sprinting out the back door $15,000 to $40,000 richer. (Dewitt's clothes would be discreetly left next to his Lincoln Continental.)[134]

As soon as Towhead White's career crossed paths with Buford Pusser, the infamous, beloved/despised, cult hero, hard-living sheriff of McNairy County, Tennessee, his days as a criminal began to wane. Or did the days of Pusser begin to wane?

The two rivals were men with similar personalities, on different sides of the law but both willing to bend the law, sleeping with the same woman in a multifaceted and taboo relationship. They lined up as opponents and began to hurl insults, threats and bullets in their dismal jousts.[135]

Hatchie River, Mississippi-Tennessee
1964

Tired of Pusser's zeal and the threat he posed to his money, Towhead White began placing menacing calls to the sheriff warning him to back off. When the threats began to come over his home line and into the ears of his wife, Pusser decided to pay his own call—at Towhead's de facto home.

When a sloshed Towhead meandered from the White Iris in Corinth toward the Shamrock Motel in Tennessee, Pusser jumped him, .41 in hand. He removed Towhead's .38, cuffed him and ordered him in the car. Pusser drove him over the border toward the Hatchie River. The sheriff took the handcuffed man to the river bottoms and "worked him over." Hours later, he dropped Towhead back off at his motel and sped off.[136]

Far from being cowed, Towhead vowed revenge. Sheriff Pusser, after all, was threatening not just his pride but also his income. The state line was his cash cow. Should word of an enthusiastic, vigilant, vigilante Tennessee sheriff permeate the region, customers might seek another establishment in which to blow off steam—and to spend (be scammed of) their money.

January 14, 1965

A woman placed a call to Pusser, urging him to bust some men working a still in some nearby woods. The sheriff sped toward the still. Towhead discreetly pulled out behind him. When Pusser parked and went into the woods, Towhead sauntered over to the sheriff's car with a gallon of gasoline and a matchbook. Pusser had to call for a ride home.[137]

February 1, 1966

Sheriff Pusser drove to the Shamrock Motel to serve a warrant on Louise Hathcock. Two travelers from Illinois bravely waited at the motel to sign the theft warrant claiming that Louise had robbed them of $125. This time there was no scam, just pure greed. She simply saw how much money her guest had in his wallet and told him to leave it all on the counter and return to Illinois. If he called the cops, he and his wife would end up in the Tennessee River.

Pusser entered the motel and informed Louise that she was under arrest for theft. While two deputies kept an eye on the infuriated matron of the state line, Pusser discovered a half case of whiskey, adding to her charges. Shocked, angry and buzzed, Louise told the sheriff that there was much more to know about her operation but that she would only tell him in private. She picked up her bourbon and coke and led Pusser to her bedroom. When they entered, she withdrew the same pistol with which Towhead had shot her husband and pointed it at a stunned Pusser, who immediately leaped back. He bounced off the door and fell onto the bed, with the bullet slamming into the wall above him. Before he could unholster his own gun, Louise put her .38 to his head and pulled the trigger; it jammed. Pusser quickly unloaded three shots into the tipsy woman's shoulder, chest and head.

Louise Hathcock, the queen of the state line mob and lover of Towhead White, was dead.[138]

New Hope Methodist Church
McNairy County, Tennessee
August 12, 1967

Sheriff Pusser drove down New Hope Road to break up a reported fight between several drunks. His wife, Pauline, rode beside him. As they passed the Methodist church and its adjoining cemetery, a black Cadillac pulled up behind them and then beside them. It lowered its windows, and .30-caliber bullets sprayed the Pusser car. Shattered glass flew into Buford's face. Soft-nosed lead slugs slammed into Pauline's face. Another round of bullets hit the sheriff himself. He took two slugs in the jaw. After radioing in an ambulance, Pusser met it on the way into Selmer, Tennessee, where Pauline was pronounced dead. He would spend the next two and a half weeks recovering in a Memphis hospital.

WALTER READE THEATRES

Community
Kingston 331-1613

SPECIAL PREVIEW SATURDAY
NIGHT ONLY — 1 SHOW 9:45
FOR MATURE AUDIENCES

**Audiences are standing up
and applauding...**

WALKING TALL

"BEST AMERICAN MOVIE OF THE YEAR!"
—Rolling Stone

CINERAMA RELEASING presents
"WALKING TALL"
Starring
JOE DON BAKER   ELIZABETH HARTMAN
ROSEMARY MURPHY   ABCP Production   In Color.
                  A service of Cox Broadcasting Corp.

Left: An advertisement for *Walking Tall*, a film about Buford Pusser, published in 1973. *Internet Archive.*

Below: A 1969 Cadillac Fleetwood Eldorado coupe. *Alden Jewell.*

Sitting in his prison cell, where he had been sentenced to three years for manufacturing and selling untaxed whiskey as well as for his role in the Biloxi casino robbery, Towhead White was comforted knowing that his adversary lay in an infirmary severely wounded.[139]

El Ray Hotel
Corinth, Mississippi
April 2, 1969

The most feared man along the Mississippi-Tennessee border unholstered his .38-caliber Smith & Wesson and took careful aim at his next victim. White was known as an expert marksman, so his target was doomed to be blown to bits. Towhead White quickly emptied five bullets across the backyard and into the house. He missed—all five times. His victim continued to hang from the ceiling, destined to provide electric light to the abandoned house for a little while longer.

Furious at failing to hit the lightbulb, a recently paroled and drunk Towhead White ordered his latest fling, Shirley Smith, to get in his brand-new green Chrysler. The two hurtled down U.S. 72 to Arnold's Truck Stop for some food to soak up the alcohol. The couple ordered two fried catfish plates and then headed back to their car. Before leaving, Shirley placed a call from the stop's phone booth.

Minutes later, the two were once again roaring down U.S. 72 to the El Ray Motel, an expensive gold watch on his wrist, a diamond ring on his finger and a canvas bag of quarters in the back seat.[140] Waiting for him atop the roof of the motel lay a sniper with a .30-.30 rifle.

On April 4, 1969, Towhead White was laid to rest. His soul left his body behind in his expensive green 1969 Chrysler. His body was placed in a coffin six feet underground, without his ring, his watch or his money—the mammon for which he gave his life.[141]

Chapter 14

STAVE MAD

William Dunbar, Cruel Taskmaster

1773

William Dunbar steered his raft, carried along by the Father of Waters, into the hot, wet, diseased and unsettled South. Dunbar looked at the towering oak trees around him and couldn't help but see money, each tree falling and shattering in his mind into neat, geometric shapes. Staves—Dunbar would become the god of staves, and his Jamaican slaves would make his vision real. Dunbar would turn all these forests to staves, and damn the Jamaicans.

He was only twenty-three, a native of Scotland and college educated. He came from a respected family and immigrated to America with £1,000 to his name. He was curious, brash and hell-bent on getting rich in the New World.[142]

Dunbar began his life in America in Philadelphia in 1771. Immediately, he looked west to the frontier. He would make his fortune out there, he thought. He transported the trade goods he had brought from London over the Appalachians to Pittsburgh, at the time a hub of Indian trade, still being settled by fortune seekers. He tried his hand at the fur trade in the wilderness of Western Pennsylvania. He would disappear into the woods and return with pelts. He hated it. But he saved some cash and borrowed more from a fellow trader. The money would buy a lot of land down south, far down the Ohio River. Even far down the Mississippi River.[143] Dunbar had a scientific mind, and he felt sure he could get rich planting.

Pittsburgh, sketched by Joseph Warin in 1796. *New York Public Library.*

Dunbar loaded his possessions onto a crude raft and floated them down the Ohio and Mississippi Rivers. He landed at Manchac, an area of British West Florida south of Natchez. Natchez at the time was a rough frontier outpost—just a river landing with a dozen rough buildings "under the hill" and a few dozen settler families farming in the vicinity. Manchac was a promising riverfront settlement that offered access to trade, transportation and fertile soil, but it was also a steamy, undeveloped swampland populated by rattlesnakes, rats, mosquitoes and enthusiastic pathogens.

Dunbar set his eyes on one thousand acres there and devised a plan; he would sail to Jamaica and purchase slaves. Then he would sail to Pensacola and ask Governor Peter Chester for a land grant—*I have all these slaves, see? I just need good land to plant.*

He bought the slaves. But while he was in Jamaica, he had a new idea. Everything seemed to be stored in wooden barrels. Manchac was overrun with hardwood trees. Could Dunbar shift his plans, harvest what was already there rather than plant anew?

In Pensacola, Chester granted his request. Dunbar returned to Manchac in 1773 by way of a series of lakes and rivers.[144]

By 1776, Dunbar had established himself in that frontier land, at least somewhat; he had a home there, and he was in the process of building houses for his slaves.

William Dunbar. *Josh Foreman.*

Dunbar shared the land with the enslaved people who were bound to labor for him. In May 1776, when he began keeping a detailed daily account of the work on his plantation, he owned fourteen "plantation negroes" who worked in the field and kept his house. He also owned twenty-three "new negroes" whom Dunbar was in the process of selling but who worked on his plantation as well.[145]

Dunbar considered himself a benevolent master, but his slaves had come to know well that the opposite was true. He may have been kinder than some, but slavery was still a savage arrangement. Dunbar, driven by his vision of plantation riches, "tricked slaves into a constant one hundred percent effort," one historian wrote, "and bragged about the profits he plowed back into his holdings or carted off to the bank."[146]

The daily grind of labor on the Dunbar plantation consisted of groups of slaves tending fields, making staves or recuperating from illness.

Corn was the subsistence crop relied on in frontier Manchac. To keep the slave machine running, it had to be fed corn, and to be fed corn, the slave machine had to grow corn.

On May 27, 1776, Dunbar watched as nineteen enslaved workers lifted and dropped their hoes, weeding a field of corn that would grow into provisions. When the work of planting and weeding the corn crop was finished—for the moment—the gang would move on to a rice field. Again the hoes would rise and fall. Sometimes the gang would plant peas or pumpkins or cut sugar cane.

Then it was back to the corn—the gang would spend days "suckering" the crop, removing side branches so that the corn stalks would grow tall and produce heavy ears. Then it was back to the rice fields to thresh. Then back to the cane to cut. Day after day, rain or shine, hot or cold. Summer arrived, and temperatures climbed into the nineties.

Growing food was a necessity, but Dunbar was ultimately after fortune. Barrels were indispensable, and to make barrels, a cooper needed staves.

On any given day, a portion of Dunbar's slaves was engaged in stave-making. They would cut down red and white oak trees, saw them up into sections, split the sections and shape the wood into uniform pieces. The slaves made hundreds of staves each day, with each person employed in the task producing between one hundred and two hundred finished staves each. Dunbar carefully noted the exact number of staves produced by each slave. Unlike the job of growing corn or peas, stave-making was a job that allowed Dunbar to extract maximum labor from his slaves year-round. There was no "stave season"—there were always trees to fell and always staves to make.

Dunbar used a "division of labor" principle to organize his stave-making gangs, with different people completing different steps of the process. The work was exhausting; two of his "wenches" who'd been sawing complained that they were exhausted and asked to work in the fields as a respite. Stave-making could be dangerous too. One slave cut his foot badly with an axe. Another slave cut a finger nearly off with a hatchet.

Dunbar's workforce was never completely healthy. On many days, groups of five or six or more were too sick to work. Dunbar doesn't mention specific maladies in his journal, only referencing "ague," an "intermitting fever with cold fits succeeded by hot," that was likely malaria. Even Dunbar could not escape illness, growing too sick sometimes even to write in his journal. Sometimes a worker would die, and his or her death would be noted in only the most cursory and sparse details in Dunbar's journal: "Saturday 20th. A new negro being a natural died."[147]

Dunbar would encourage his slaves to work harder by promising the most productive a handkerchief or coat. And he would discipline them harshly when they did not meet his expectations. Two enslaved women named Ketty and Bessie ran away from Dunbar's plantation because he had given them "a little correction the former evening for disobedience." When he caught Bessie, he put her in irons for a week and then whipped her twenty-five times "as a punishment and example to the rest." When he found a slave named Adam drunk on rum, he put him in a makeshift jail, interrogated him about where he got the rum and sentenced him to five hundred lashes.[148]

Despite the challenges to keeping his enslaved workforce healthy, fed and compliant, his stave-making enterprise was astonishingly successful. The volume of staves produced grew into the hundreds of thousands; in one trip to the Mississippi River in 1777, Dunbar transported 100,000 staves ready for sale. Other frontier planters visited Dunbar to learn from his stave making operation.[149]

But Dunbar's stave-making operation was doomed to failure, though not because of anything Dunbar did. When the American Revolution began, a river pirate named James Willing sailed down the Mississippi, plundering Loyalist plantations—including Dunbar's plantation in Manchac. Willing took everything of value from Dunbar, tore down his fences and set his animals loose. Dunbar fled across the Mississippi River, into Spanish territory. When given the chance, many of his enslaved workers abandoned him, escaping in the confusion.

Dunbar, still in his twenties, did not give up on his dream of growing rich in America. Shortly after he lost his plantation in Manchac, he moved to Natchez, where he became one of the richest and most influential planters and scientists in the Mississippi Territory.[150]

Chapter 15

JOHN LAW AND THE
MISSISSIPPI BUBBLE

*J*ohn Law looked across the table at his opponent. He looked at the dice on the table and then back at the man staring curiously at him. Law wagered that his opponent could not roll six sixes in a row. He offered 10,000-to-1 odds. The man eagerly took his bet, tossed the dice and paid Law one livre. John Law knew that the odds were in his favor at 46,656-to-one and won yet another bet.

Law was a professional gambler. Having been bailed out of debtor's prison by his mother years before, he had taken to reading and studying every book and treatise on odds and gambling that he could locate. He then hit the gambling tables with a vengeance.[151]

Handsome, debonair and increasing his wealth as he circulated among the gambling tables of Scotland and England, he grew proportionately attractive to the ladies of his ever-growing circle. After killing a man in a duel over one such vixen, Law was imprisoned and sentenced to death. Through his connections, however, he was allowed to escape and made his way to France.[152] He spent the next twenty-two years carousing, gambling and, most importantly, studying every economic text he could.

When Louis XIV died, Law's connections and studies paid off. He had a new patron, the Duc d'Orleans, regent to the five-year-old heir to the throne. The new regent of a nearly bankrupt kingdom appointed Law controller of general finances. Law quickly began circulating more paper money throughout the realm. The new currency was no longer backed by gold and silver, but rather by the wealth of France's colonies that Law planned to

Mr. JEAN LAW CONer. DU ROY EN TOUS CES CONils. CONTROLEUR
GNÁL DES FINANCES en 1720.
Sous l'Auguste et Sage Regence | Law consomme dans l'art de regir la finance
D'un Prince aimant la bonne foy: | Trouve l'art d'enrichir les sujets et le Roy.

John Law. *Library of Congress.*

develop/exploit. Money was back in circulation, catapulting France from the barter system to a modern economy. Stocks were soaring. Promised riches from the New World would soon be pouring in. Law was a genius, a savior, the wolf of Paris's financial district.[153]

It seemed as if everyone in France was caught up in Law's speculative schemes. The famed philosopher Voltaire wrote:

> *It's good to come to the country where Plutus is turning all heads in the city. Have you really all gone mad in Paris? I only hear talk of millions. They say that everyone who is comfortably off is now in misery, and everyone who was impoverished revels in opulence. Is this reality? Is this a chimera? Has half of the nation found the philosopher's stone in the paper mills? Is John Law a god, a rogue, or a charlatan who is poisoning himself with the drug he is distributing to everyone?*[154]

John Law had turned himself into the second-most powerful man in France. He then turned his attention to the riches of a continent. He acquired a tobacco company in 1718 and then the Company of Senegal and the Company of Saint-Domingue, thereby cornering the slave market. One year later, his bank was nationalized as the Banque Royale, and he acquired the East India Company and the Company of the Indies. At its peak, Law's bank and company's shares of 1,000 livres were selling at 10,000 livres.[155]

By now, Law was under pressure to validate his stocks. He needed to back his paper money with some sort of specie. And so, he founded the Company of the West, which soon merged with the East India Company and rebranded itself as the Company of the Indies or, popularly, the Mississippi Company. Law was given a twenty-five-year lease to develop concessions (plantations) along the Mississippi River that would produce cash crops that would revitalize the French economy and make France once again the most powerful nation in Europe.

Law's charter made him the de facto king of Louisiana, with the power to tax and make war, as well as all other powers consistent with a totalitarian state. In exchange, he promised to populate Louisiana with six thousand settlers and three thousand Africans.[156]

All Law needed now to turn his great gamble into a fiscally solvent nation was to populate a continent 7,500 miles away.

Portrait of Mary Sylvester, an early American woman (1754). *Metropolitan Museum of Art.*

THE PROMISES

The Company of the Indies distributed a series of fliers throughout France and parts of Germany encouraging citizens to immigrate to Louisiana. One such poster promised:

> *The climate is very mild and temperate. A good air is breathed in it, and one feels a perpetual spring, which contributes much to the fertility of the country which abounds in all things….*
>
> *Above the Mississippi there are mountains full of gold, silver, copper, lead, and quicksilver, which favor commerce, for the savages have become so much acquainted with the French colonies that they trade in good faith without distrusting or fearing on either side.*[157]

Another such advertisement promised that the countryside of the Mississippi Company was "[a] land of milk and honey in which the climate was temperate, the soil fertile, the woods replete with trees suited to building and export, and the countryside populated with wild yet benign 'horses, buffaloes, and cows, which however do not harm but run away at the sight of men.'"[158]

And then there was the silver and jewels produced by the abundant mines, not to mention the beautiful landscape: French castles and hamlets filled with cottages, each overlooking 120 acres of land requiring minimal labor. And then there were the rivers and hills and mountains. (Yes, mountains; go ahead and laugh, residents of Louisiana and Mississippi.[159])

When the carrot failed to work, Law turned to the stick—or, in this case, the law. An army of archers was sent into the streets of Paris in search of undesirables and unemployed. With a promised bounty of 100 livres per captive, the special police force had no problem filling the jails of Paris with "vagrants"—some legitimate, others in the wrong place at the wrong time—who would then be given an unenviable choice: rot in a Parisian prison or migrate to Louisiana. A repeat of Nero's Christian persecutions and a foreshadowing of American McCarthyism, neighbor turned on neighbor, denouncing rivals and ridding themselves of foes.

In September 1719, eighty criminals received a conditional reprieve, were publicly wedded to eighty prostitutes—the couples chained together—and marched to the ship that would carry them to Biloxi.[160] Similar weddings followed. French citizens began equating Louisiana with a penal colony. Some of those condemned to exportation began to rebel. Riots spread throughout the country. Finally, in 1720, forced deportations—at the request of Louisiana officials, the condemned and concerned citizens—officially ground to a halt.

THE REALITY

The first phase of the colonists' relocation to Louisiana was a trip to the French coast, where most of the emigrants, willing and unwilling, waited weeks or months for their ships to be ready. Law's Company of the Mississippi erected tent cities on the wharves and public spaces of the port towns but failed to provide sufficient food or medicine. In one town, Lorient, half of the four thousand would-be colonists died of cholera before even boarding their transports. One of the ships leaving Lorient missed a cholera patient, causing another half of the colonists to die en route.

Between 1717 and 1721, 7,000 colonists arrived in Louisiana; 2,000 either died on the sea journey or immediately defected to rival colonies upon landing. And then half of the remaining 5,000 died before they ever reached their assigned concession. The Germans fared even worse. Only 300 of the original 1,300 passengers made it to their destination.[161]

Those who survived the transatlantic voyage landed not in Paradiso but Inferno. They had replaced one tent city on the coasts of France for another in Biloxi; only the latter camp was cursed with bitterly cold winds during the winter months and oppressively humid weather in the summer. Then there were the alligators and sand fleas, the rats and mosquitoes. There was infertile land, hunger and, all too often, death.

Many of the passengers never made it to Biloxi. They died twelve miles offshore on Ship Island. Biloxi's port was not deep enough to harbor incoming ships, and so most of the cargo, trade and human, was deposited at Ship Island and then rowed inland. Whenever one of Biloxi's frequent epidemics broke out, passengers were quarantined on Ship Island—often for weeks, sometimes for months, on occasion in perpetuity (burned rather than buried due to sandy soil and the ever-present rats).[162]

Those who made it to Biloxi expected prompt transport to their assigned concessions, their cottages and their 120 acres of fertile land. They received none of those. The ships' supplies were pilfered and distributed to the capital's bureaucrats and soldiers. The new arrivals lived off whatever they could fish from the sea (many of the German settlers died from an overreliance on raw oysters)[163] or trade from the Natives, who, rather than being docile and willing servants, were just as eager to turn a profit as their European counterparts.

Food shortages became so severe that many of the French soldiers were given leave to live inland among the Native tribes during the coastal famines. But still the emigrants continued to arrive, sent by John Law, who was determined to meet his promised quota of 6,000 citizens and 3,000 Africans. The added personnel put further strain on a dwindling food supply. The situation was so dire that the valuable slaves were sold at bargain prices. And still they came, both colonists and slaves. (By 1721, 1,900 slaves were dispersed throughout Louisiana from Biloxi.[164] The number of slaves would reach 3,600 by 1732, doubling the number of French residents.)[165]

French explorer and naturalist Antoine-Simon Le Page du Pratz summed up conditions in Biloxi in 1721:

> *Nothing but fine sand, as white and shining as snow, on which no kinds of greens can be raised; besides, the being extremely incommoded with rats, which swarm there in the sand, and at that time even ate the very stocks of the guns, the famine being there so very great, that more than five hundred people died of hunger, bread being very dear, and flesh-meat still more rare....*[The deprivation was due to] *the arrival of several grantees all at once; so as to have neither provisions, nor boats to transport them to the places of their destination, as the company has obliged them to do.*[166]

Left to their own devices, most of the colonists had to make their own way to the concessions Law had promised them. Many died along the way or shortly after, arriving sick and weakened by their ordeals in France, over the Atlantic and in Biloxi.

Enough settlers overcame the poor planning, corruption and greed of America's first and Europe's largest land scheme to date and survived to become the co-progenitors of Mississippi.

LAW'S ENTIRE SCHEME HINGED on making Louisiana a financial success. The wealth of the New World was to pay the debts of the Old. But first Louisiana required settlers, and those settlers needed to turn a quick profit in raw goods. Neither materialized. Louisiana remained depopulated and never came close to rivaling Spain's export of valuable minerals or

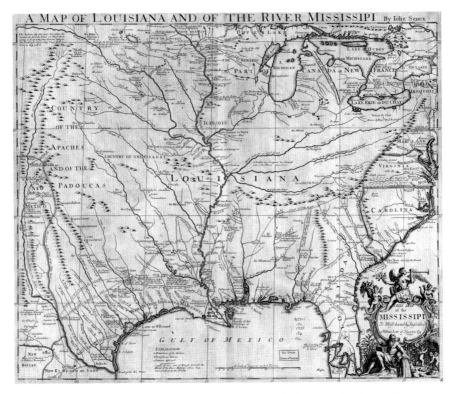

This map, taken from the New General Atlas of 1721, is dedicated to Mr. Law. It is a translation of the French map of Delisle, published in 1718. *Library of Congress.*

Britain's agricultural exports. In short, the Mississippi Company was an economic failure.

In the hopes of delaying bankruptcy and buying the Mississippi concessions time to turn profitable, Law began printing an excess of paper money. When investors began to demand that their notes be redeemed as specie, Law temporarily closed the Banque Royal and began confiscating precious metals. More and more panicked investors flocked to the bank seeking to redeem their notes. When an official returned from Louisiana disputing official propaganda that claimed Louisiana was full of emeralds and silver, he was promptly imprisoned.[167] Soon a general panic erupted, followed by a European panic.

Law's scheming came to an end in 1720 when the Duc d'Orleans dismissed the Scotsman, who promptly fled the country. Shortly after, the Mississippi Company shares that had been selling at 10,000 livres/share was down to 500 livres/share. Untold investors were now bankrupt. The Banque

Royal and the Mississippi Company were in ruins. Angry and hungry mobs attacked financiers and bankers. They sought Law's head, but he was already gone. They turned their fury on the Duc d'Orleans. When the regent died two years later, rumors began circulating that, upon his death, his Great Dane leaped into his bed and ate his heart—a fitting end for the greedy monster who impoverished France.[168]

WHETHER LAW WAS A brilliant economic theorist or a cynical opportunist is a question the current authors leave for far more qualified economists. From a historical and human perspective, there is no question that his scheme to bring France out of debt by relying on the riches of Louisiana led to an exponential rise of speculators, traders and those looking to earn a "fast livre." The desire to earn without working has fueled many a scheme, and countless more fall victim to the promise of wealth without work, from lottery tickets to jackpot justice to slum landlords to FTX and countless other empty promises of easy wealth. As long as these promises are made, human persons will greedily line up for easy money.

Greed popped the Mississippi Bubble. Greed has doomed many a nation—and legions of souls.

GLUTTONY

· ·

Wine is a mocker, strong drink is a brawler,
and whoever is led astray by it is not wise.
—Proverbs 20:1

…for my sin of gluttony I am damned,
as you can see, to rain that beats me weak.
And my sad sunken soul is not alone,
for all these sinners here share in my pain
and in my sin.
—Dante, Inferno *VI, 52–57*

Chapter 16

SODDEN STORIES FROM
MISSISSIPPI'S "DRY" AGE, 1908–1966

Jackson, Mississippi
February 4, 1966

It was a frigid day in Jackson, Mississippi. The low would drop to twenty degrees Fahrenheit.[169] And yet the hottest social event of the year would take place that evening: the Carnival Ball. The seat of Deputy Sheriff Tom Shelton was also growing hotter by the day. The teetotaler had just replaced his boss, Sheriff Fred Pickett, who had been placed on indefinite leave for habitual drunkenness. Determined to uphold the law and enforce state prohibition, Shelton promptly began raiding bootlegging establishments. Most of his raids occurred among the poor or the Black sections of Jackson, leading many to accuse the deputy of selectively and politically choosing his targets. Wanting to clean up the reputation of an office known for hypocrisy, Shelton decided to set his sights higher: he would raid the headquarters of Mississippi's elite: the Jackson Country Club.

In 1966, thirty-three years after the federal repeal of Prohibition, Mississippi was still a dry state—likely the wettest dry state in the nation. Liquor was illegal, unless you paid an official black market tax. The confusion caused by Mississippians' abstentious and gluttonous attitude toward alcohol was bringing in much-needed revenue by charging a 10 percent tax on the illegal product, but it was also costing the state out-of-state investments in business, tourism and conventions, as few could unravel the intricacies of Mississippi's official policy toward alcohol. The state's back-and-forth attitude toward spirits was an embarrassment,[170] so much so that Governor Paul Johnson Jr. urged his fellow Mississippians to do the sensible thing and finally repeal the Volstead Act:

> *It is high time for someone to stand boldly at the front door and talk plainly, sensibly and honestly about whiskey, black-market taxes, payola, and all of the many-colored hues that make up Mississippi's illegal aurora borealis of prohibition.*[171]

Like the rest of the nation, Mississippi's experiment with prohibition had been an abject failure. Now, after nearly six decades, Governor Johnson was suggesting that the "noble experiment" be concluded. Two days after asking his fellow Mississippians to reflect on their collective hypocritical attitude toward alcohol, he put on his suit and tie and prepared to attend the Carnival Ball—and then the after party at the Jackson Country Club.

Greenwood, Mississippi
August 13, 1938

Ralph "R.D." Davis was furious when he heard the news. His wife, Beatrice, was sleeping with the young bluesman who had just come to town. The man had a few recordings and had been to New York City. Now he was staying in Baptist Town over in Greenwood—the same Baptist Town where Beatrice's sister lived, the sister she had been visiting every Monday for the last month. Or so R.D. thought. Now he knew.

He also knew that the guitarist was going to be playing at Three Forks—the store and juke joint located where Highway 82 intersects 49E. It was the same juke R.D. worked at on weekends, handing out corn liquor to eager customers. He knew the musician's reputation for drink. Everyone knew the man's weakness for alcohol. R.D. decided to act.

Saturday night came around, and the juke filled up. The bluesman strummed his guitar and crooned as if it would be his last performance. In between songs, he chugged liquor, as was his custom. Meanwhile, R.D. was preparing a special drink for the womanizer. He gave his wife, the guitarist's lover, a jar full of corn liquor in which he had dissolved several mothballs. The odorless, tasteless naphthalene would make the man nauseous and gaseous. Then the stomach cramps would set in, followed by vomiting. The man who had turned R.D. into a cuckold would be publicly humiliated and

"Barred." By Nan Lurie, sponsored by the Works Progress Administration (circa 1938). *New York Public Library.*

then confined to bed for a few days. Then R.D. would confront his wife. The community would know that no one makes a fool of R.D.

As expected, his nemesis drank the whiskey. He continued to play a little while longer and then stopped. More and more people entered the juke hoping to hear the famous bluesman, but he sat in a corner, guitar under his arm, claiming to be too sick. But the crowds wanted music. He tried again but then stumbled off stage. For the next three days, he tossed and turned and howled and vomited blood, as the varices in his esophagus erupted. Choking on his own blood and quickly bleeding out, Robert Johnson—rambler, womanizer, alcoholic, genius—died alone.[172]

Rankin County
August 27, 1946

Constable Norris Overby sauntered into the Spot, grabbed a bottle of liquor and abruptly left the nightclub. Overby was on the sheriff's payroll and was accustomed to the alcohol freebies along Mississippi's "Gold Coast"—East Jackson and Rankin County—where gambling, prostitution, bootlegging and crime ran rampant. Rumors circulated that between the black market tax and protection money, the sheriff was the highest-paid official in the state. Those working for him were accustomed to looking the other way and being rewarded for it. On this day, though, Constable Overby made a fatal miscalculation. He had just "stolen" from a club belonging to the volatile Sam Seaney.

As soon as Overby left the Spot, the bartender called his boss, Sam Seaney, who was working his other club, Shady Rest, just one hundred yards away, and informed him of Overby's heist/extortion. Seaney was no friend of the law. He paid his bribes and hush money but secretly seethed with each payment rendered. He was arrested in 1935 for selling illegal liquor. His club, The Jeep, was padlocked in 1937 for the same offense. When Seaney busted the padlock and resumed business, he was fined $1,000. By 1939, he had opened the Spot and Shady Rest, both near his own house. Not long after, his new clubs were raided by 150 National Guardsmen in the largest raid to date on the Gold Coast. Twenty-one bars yielded eighty-five slot machines, twenty-nine gaming tables and forty-one arrests, including Sam Seaney, his brother and their father. Seaney's solution was to make bail, pay more protection money and continue with his lucrative business.[173]

"Drunken Silenus." By Jonas Suderhoef (circa 1630–50). *Metropolitan Museum of Art.*

Five years later, Seaney found himself on the end of another shakedown—this time by Norris Overby. Two days prior, Overby had raided the Spot and demanded that Seaney shut the club down by the end of the week. Seaney refused, and now he was on the phone listening to his bartender relate another Overby slight.

As luck would have it, Overby then walked into Shady Rest, bottle of liquor in tow. The constable walked in the front door, past the bar, into the red-carpeted, mirrored hallway and up the four steps that led to the dance floor.

Seaney let him go no farther, and the two erupted into a heated argument. Both drew their pistols and commenced firing, almost simultaneously. Overby fell where he stood at the top of the stairs, while Seaney tumbled to the bottom of the stairs. Wounded but alive, the two men fired at each other again. Sheriff H.G. Laird later explained: "The two men met in the doorway of Seaney's dance establishment crowded with 400 patrons, scuffled, drew guns, fired, and fell wounded….From their positions on the floor…they continued the duel [with Seaney shooting Overby] through the chest" and Overby putting a bullet "through Seaney's body near the heart."[174]

The shootout at Shady Rest left two men dead but, miraculously, none wounded. It also garnered national attention and reminded Mississippians of the dangers of mixing weapons and alcohol. Soon after, local outcry caused the local law enforcement to seriously crack down on the sale of spirits.

Corinth, Mississippi
June 20, 1964

Towhead White was drunk. Again. He was sitting in a booth at the Shamrock Restaurant arguing with his lover, Louise Hathcock. At a nearby table sat the only gangster along the state line who might challenge him, Tommy Bivens. Bivens was chatting with friends when White suddenly called him out. He accused Bivens of being a coward and informed him that he would shortly receive a long-overdue beating. There could only be one cock-of-the walk along the state line.

Bivens recognized that his old partner and friend was hammered. He tried to defuse the situation but must have known it was fruitless. Before the night was over, and likely sooner than later, he would be fighting his inebriated friend. It was sooner.

White leaped from his chair and proceeded to pound Bivens's face with his fists while the latter was still seated in the booth. The more sober Bivens finally gained his feet and proceeded to land several punches to White's face, drawing blood in the process. A frantic Louise begged Bivens to stop and tugged on White, pleading with him to follow her to her room. The couple, who five minutes earlier were in a heated argument, left the lounge. An exasperated Bivens sat down, frustrated and angry with his drunk partner.

Five minutes later, White burst in the back door, .38 in hand, and fired at Bivens's head. Instinctively, Biven turned, and the bullet tore through the left side of his nose out through his right cheek. The couple he had been speaking with rushed him to the hospital. An intoxicated White fled the premises and soon crashed his Cadillac into a tree. A Good Samaritan chauffeured White to the hospital.

Neither Bivens nor White would serve time. The incident had simply been another liquor-induced Mississippi feud.[175]

DEPUTY SHELTON ENTERED THE Jackson Country Club while the Carnival Ball was in full swing downtown at the Coliseum. He demanded that the bartender, Charles Wood, hand over his illegal liquor. Wood immediately called his boss, Ed Brunini, the president of the country club, who promptly drove over to confront Shelton. By the time Brunini arrived, Shelton had found the champagne, but he wanted more. He wanted the club's wine

Cartoon by Bert Hansen showing men buying "patent medicines" at a Georgia train station during the onset of Prohibition. *Beinecke Library at Yale University.*

and liquor stash as well. Brunini then informed the deputy that he was an uninvited intruder and that he would not be assisting him in any way. Shelton and his men searched the premises and found nothing. Convinced that the rest of the spirits were behind the locked bar, he demanded the key. He was refused.

By that time, the new acting sheriff realized that he had shown up to a liquor raid without an axe. He and his deputies had no choice but to go back to the station in search of one. By the time he returned, the after party had begun. The determined Shelton marched back to the bar and proceeded to batter down the door and remove the liquor.

With the amused and angry cream of Jackson society looking on, including Governor Paul Johnson Jr., Shelton marched out with the party's alcohol—more than 1,200 bottles of various spirits. Marching alongside the deputy sheriff was the only man arrested that night: the bar manager, Charles Wood.[176]

The aftermath of the Jackson Country Club raid was predictable. Needless to say, quite a few of the state's most powerful lawyers were present at the raid. Charles Wood had no problem assembling a dream team of defense attorneys, and they promptly sued the State of Mississippi for its absurd alcohol laws. Wood was soon acquitted. Six months later, state-enforced prohibition officially ended in Mississippi.

Chapter 17

ULYSSES GRANT'S
YAZOO RIVER BINGE

Haynes' Bluff, Fourteen Miles Northwest of Vicksburg
June 5, 1863

The vise around Vicksburg was closing. General Ulysses S. Grant, commander of the Mississippi Department, had met with failure after failure in his attempt to subdue the Gibraltar of the Confederacy. But now his troops were in position. The fate of Vicksburg was sealed. Only two obstacles stood in the way: a Rebel relief army and alcohol.

Rumors soon reached Union headquarters: Confederate general Joseph Johnston was just thirty miles away, up the Yazoo River in Satartia. General Grant decided to reconnoiter. With just a few aides, he boarded the USS *Diligence* and thus began what would become one of history's most controversial joy rides. He left behind a tent with a case of wine at the entrance and several empty bottles inside.

ULYSSES GRANT BEGAN DRINKING heavily after the war with Mexico. A concerned soldier-friend wrote home that Grant was "altered very much: he is a short thick man with a beard reaching half way down his waist and I fear he drinks too much but don't you say a word on that subject."[177] Another friend added that Grant "got to drinking heavily during or after the war. [He] was in bad shape from the effects of drinking, and suffering from *mania a potu* [delirium tremens] and some other troubles of the campaign."[178]

Ulysses S. Grant. *Library of Congress.*

Marriage and fatherhood seemed to have a positive effect on the promising officer. Back in the Midwest, he made a sincere and serious attempt to settle down, even meeting with his Methodist minister about his issues with the bottle. After hearing his pastor's advice, Grant took the pledge and promised to henceforth foreswear the bottle.[179] He even helped to open a Sons of Temperance lodge.[180]

When war erupted between the states, Grant cast his lot with the Union. Quickly earning a reputation as a fighter, Grant rose in the estimation of President Lincoln, who had a poor track record of promoting indecisive, overly cautious commanders who seemed to relish inaction. Grant was different—he *fought*. But he also drank. Worse, he could not hold his alcohol.

Grant's drinking is a hotly debated topic among Civil War historians, as it was among his contemporaries. Those who hated Grant—and there were plenty—accused of being a perpetual sot. And those who adored him—and there were just as many—swore that he never touched spirits. The truth likely lies somewhere in between. An enemy like the editor of the *Cincinnati Commercial* could write to the secretary of the treasury:

You do once in a while, don't you say a word to the President, or Stanton, or Halleck, about the conduct of the war? Well, now, for God's sake say that Genl Grant, entrusted with our greatest army, is a jackass in the original package. He is a poor drunken imbecile. He is a poor stick sober, and he is most of the time more than half drunk, and much of the time idiotically drunk.[181]

On the other hand, an admirer such as Mary Livermore, leader of a Sanitary Commission, could write that Grant had "clear eye, clean skin, firm flesh, and steady nerves…gave the lie to the universal calumnies then current concerning his intemperate habits."[182]

Regardless, enough accusations reached Lincoln that the president had no choice but to investigate. In the end, he decided that he could not replace Grant. When approached by a delegation concerned with the General's drinking, Lincoln replied, "If I knew what brand of whiskey he drinks I would send a barrel or so to some other generals."[183]

Grant seems to have been one of those drinkers who could abstain. He would go long periods without touching alcohol. He would sit through official dinners with his glass overturned, not taking even a sip. His conservative Methodist conscience caused him great pain when he did imbibe, and throughout the war, he would make sure that his devoted wife was nearby. He also kept the ever-watchful teetotaler John Rawlins on his staff for both his talent as an organizer and for his vigilant dedication to keeping his general on the straight and narrow. In short, Grant knew that he had a drinking problem and fought to contain it. But once he started drinking….

The Union's most effective general could not hold his liquor, nor could he easily stop once he began. A drink with an old comrade inevitably became two, then three, then so many he was viciously hungover the following morning. These bouts did not happen often, but when they did, Grant became unpredictable, as one of his general's would write home:

He tries to let liquor alone but he cannot resist the temptation always. When he came to Memphis he left his wife at LaGrange, and for several days after getting here was beastly drunk, utterly incapable of doing anything. Quinby and I took him in charge, watching him day and night and keeping liquor away from him.…We telegraphed his wife and brought her on to take care of him.[184]

Noted Grant scholar Ron Chernow offered perhaps the fairest assessment of Grant's drinking. He never let it interfere with his duties. Nor did he allow any but a select few see him drunk. Instead, he preferred to imbibe, and imbibe heavily, at the end of long, stressful periods—especially when his wife was not around. Then, Grant's drinking became problematic.[185] But if winning a war was at the forefront of President Lincoln's mind—and it was—then standing by Grant was a wise decision.

Yazoo River
June 6, 1863

Once aboard the USS *Diligence*, General Grant began to drink. He went to the downstairs bar. He made a second trip and then a third. Soon Grant was drunk. Charles Dana, investigator for Lincoln turned Grant ally, later reported that Grant, on the "excursion of the Yazoo [was] as stupidly drunk as the immortal nature of man would allow; but the next day he came out as fresh as a rose, without any trace or indication of the spree he had passed through."[186] During the night, Dana learned from two retreating gunboats that Confederate forces had infiltrated the area around Satartia. Dana took it upon himself to retreat and return to Haynes' Bluff.

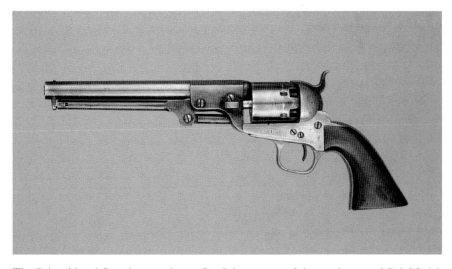

The Griswold and Gunnison revolver, a Confederate copy of the much-coveted Colt Model 1851. The Griswold and Gunnison was manufactured in Georgia from 1862 to 1864. *Metropolitan Museum of Art.*

In the morning, Grant assumed that he was in Satartia—evidence that he likely blacked out the night before. What happened during the next twenty-four hours remains a mystery. (What happens on the Yazoo River stays on the Yazoo River.) One of the newsmen closest to Grant, Sylvanus Cadwallader, published a fascinating tale of a binge, a hangover breakfast, a midafternoon booze session, a late afternoon joyride on a horse named "Kangaroo" (foreshadowing his later arrest in Washington, D.C., for riding through town at excessive speeds), passing out in a field, reluctantly riding home in the back of an ambulance to sober up and arriving back at his headquarters sober and alert, as if nothing had transpired the previous two days.

Or Grant might have just overindulged again after a period of great stress and blacked out aboard ship, regaining his senses and sense of place in the morning.

Whatever happened on the Yazoo River on June 6, 1863, three days later, Grant invited his ever faithful, devoted and vigilant wife to join him in Vicksburg for the remainder of the campaign.[187]

Chapter 18

CRAIG CLAIBORNE'S THIRTY-ONE-DISH MEAL

Chez Denis, Paris, France
1975

Mississippi native and *New York Times* food critic Craig Claiborne and his friend and fellow critic Pierre Franey took their seats at Chez Denis, a favorite haunt of food critics, near the Arc de Triomphe. The pair sat down, and over the next five hours, the following thirty-one dishes and nine wines were brought to the culinary aficionados:

Hors d'oeuvre:

beluga caviar in crystal, enclosed in shaved ice with toast

First course:

consommé Denis;
creme Andalouse [a creamy celery, tomato, and onion soup]*;*
cold germiny [a sorrel soup]*;*
parfait of sweetbreads;
mousse of quail in a small tarte;
tarte of Italian ham, mushrooms and a border of truffles;
Belon oysters broiled quickly in the shell and served with a pure beurre blanc;

lobster in a creamy, cardinal-red sauce that was heavily laden with chopped truffles;

Provençale pie made with red mullet and baked with tomato, black olives and herbs, including fennel or anise seed, rosemary, sage and thyme;

"fillet" strips of chicken plus the "oysters" found in the after backbone of chicken blended in cream sauce containing sliced wild mushrooms;

chartreuse of partridge;

tender rare-roasted fillet of Limousin beef with a rich truffle sauce;

sherbets in three flavors—raspberry, orange and lemon;

Second course:

ortolans en brochette [a small, fat songbird eaten whole];

fillets of wild duck en salmis in a rich brown game sauce;

rognonade de veau, or roasted boned loin of veal wrapped in puff pastry with fresh black truffles;

pommes Anna—the potatoes cut into small rounds and baked in butter;

purée of artichokes;

butter-rich fresh foie gras in clear aspic

Woodcock and Pheasant;

breast meat of woodcocks that was cooked until rare and served with a natural chaudfroid;

cold pheasant with fresh hazelnuts;

a cold glazed charlotte with strawberries;

ile flottante ["floating island"—meringue on vanilla custard];

poires alma [spiced baked apples, pears and mandarin];

Third course:

four pastry confections and fruits;

coffee

Wines:

1966 Champagne Comtesse Marie de France

1918 Chateau Latour

1969 Montrachet Baron Thenard

1928 Chateau Mouton Rothschild

1947 Chateau Lafite-Rothschild

1961 Chateau Petrus
1929 Romanée Conti
1928 Chateau d'Yquem
1835 madeira
choice of a 100-year-old calvados or an hors d'age cognac[188]

Upon the dinner's conclusion, when asked if he had just eaten the perfect meal, Claiborne's response was surprising and brusque: "No."

BORN AND RAISED IN Sunflower in the Mississippi Delta, Craig Claiborne developed an early love of food in his mother's kitchen. Yet his homegrown Delta palate would soon expand as he began to travel the world. Claiborne served in the navy during World War II and the Korean War but realized that life as a career serviceman did not appeal to him. His real passion was food. He took a job as a reporter, and his talent with words and descriptions quickly saw him rise to the very top of the culinary world. He became the food columnist for the *New York Times* and after decades of critiques came to be regarded as the most influential food critic in the United States. (A 2012 book was appropriately titled *The Man Who Changed the Way We Eat: Craig Claiborne and the American Food Renaissance*.)

Claiborne was a harsh critic who did not mince words. He was insistent on a holistic dining experience: taste, presentation and ambience. A fair judge of food who contributed greatly to Americans' understanding of cuisine in general, he was nonetheless, at the same time, a voracious and dainty eater with a demanding palate.

New York City
June 1974

Craig Claiborne placed the winning bid on a dinner for two at the restaurant of his choice, paid for by the item's sponsor, American Express credit cards. Claiborne's bid? $300.

Claiborne and his friend Pierre Franey immediately began salivating at their good fortune. They began checking off restaurants all over the world that they enjoyed or would like to enjoy. In the end, they decided on Chez Denis in Paris. However, not wanting to make a mistake with this once-in-a-lifetime meal, they decided to give Chez Denis a trial run.

Craig Claiborne in 1975. *Library of Congress.*

The trial was a success. Claiborne told the chef that he would return and asked for "the finest dinner in Europe," reassuring the chef that money was no issue. Denis Lahana assured him that the meal would meet his expectations.

St. Denis, Paris
November 1975

It did not. While Claiborne acknowledged that most of the food was delicious, there were too many lukewarm, chewy and improperly cooked dishes. The presentation was often lacking. The price seemed higher than expected. And there were plastic flowers in different locations throughout the restaurant.

However, Claiborne ended his critique on a generous note: "We reminded ourselves of one thing during the course of that evening: If you were Henry VIII, Lucullus, Gargantua and Bacchus, all rolled into one, you cannot possibly sustain, start to finish, a state of ecstasy while dining on a series of 31 dishes."[189]

Many around the world, including Pope Paul VI, were much more critical of the critic, calling out his gluttonous meal and its exorbitant price when so many in the world were hungry. One French critic pointed out that his meal cost what a working man often made with an entire year of labor, while the Vatican called the meal "scandalous." An American columnist added, "This calculated evening of high-class piggery *offends* an average American's sense of decency. It seems wrong morally, aesthetically and in every other way."[190]

It is unlikely that Craig Claiborne took much notice of his detractors. He continued with his mission to inform, instruct, critique and eat.[191]

LUST

···

But each person is tempted when he is lured and enticed by his own desire.
Then desire when it has conceived gives birth to sin, and sin when it is fully
grown brings forth death.
—James 1:14–15

I learned that to this place of punishment
all those who sin in lust have been condemned,
those who make reason slave to appetite.
—Dante, Inferno *V, 37–39*

Chapter 19

NELLIE JACKSON AND NATCHEZ'S MOST FAMOUS BORDELLO

Natchez, Mississippi
July 6, 1990

The Natchez Fire Department arrived at 416 North Rankin Street in the early morning hours of a humid July morning. The porch was already ablaze. So was the front room. One body stood aflame beside the road frantically waving its arms—another was inside the house. Both were alive as they burned. Although they had no way of knowing at the time, because both bodies were burned beyond recognition, one was the charred and living remains of a twenty-year-old white male. The other was an eighty-seven-year-old Black woman.

How the two unlikely acquaintances came to be burned alive on the same porch in the July darkness was a mystery quickly solved by local investigators. It was also a story that would shake the tight-knit Natchez community to its foundations.[192]

Natchez
1920s–1957

Nellie Jackson arrived in Natchez from Possum Corner, Mississippi, in the 1920s. A Black woman of charm and intelligence but no known practical skills living in the segregated Jim Crow South had little means to advance herself. Nellie was determined to use whatever means she had. She began bootlegging in Natchez-Under-the-Hill, one of the most notorious strips of land in the United States, known for its gambling, fighting, drinking and prostitution. Nellie fit right in. She was quickly picked up on a bootlegging charge and sentenced to thirty days in jail and a $100 fine.[193]

But she had learned. She would be a success, and she was determined to avoid prison in the future. Natchez offered plenty of other pleasurable and illegal opportunities. Tony Byrne, who served as mayor from 1968 to 1988, explained: "It's the oldest city on the river. There's always been gambling, prostitution, drinking and religion. It's very cosmopolitan for its size. Natchez is a river city, and anything on the river is different."[194]

By 1930, Nellie had bought a house over the bluff near the center of town. It was a homely white house with red trim around the doors. A metal cutout hung out front of a man in a hat bowing before a woman in a hoopskirt—a nostalgic reminder of the beauty (and availability) of a southern belle. Jackson clearly understood her new town. She decorated the inside with a jukebox, table and couches. But the *raison d'etre* of her new house were the beds in the extra rooms.

Her extra rooms were soon filled with female boarders. After a while, there would be a new set of boarders and then another batch. Always women. Pretty women. Asian women, Black women, white women, women from Germany and Japan and Vietnam.[195] Women who paid her rent, plus half of whatever they made in their rooms.[196]

Nellie Jackson's house. *Penelope Rose O. Starrett.*

Soon Nellie's house was known to most of Natchez. Few ever used her front door. Her big-shot guests would enter by a side door, but most entered through the back and either hung out in the kitchen or moved to the living room. Nellie's boarders would then come out and socialize with her guests.

Nellie was beginning to entertain a great number of guests, some local, some out-of-towners. When World War II erupted and recruits from Camp Van Dorn were allowed leave in town, her house was perpetually entertaining.[197] Whenever a new batch of boarders arrived, Nellie made sure to take them shopping at three or four different stores in town so that word would get out: new girls are in town. She even began to print shirts with the slogan "Follow Me to Nellie's." Her shirts spread across the country, and her clientele continued to flock to her home in Natchez. Mayor Bryne told a reporter, "Everybody had a t-shirt. All the locals wanted one. I still have my original one she gave me."[198]

Business was booming. Nellie's rules were few but firm: no drugs, no drunks and no Black customers.[199]

Natchez
June 2, 1957

Thirty-nine-year-old Estelle Hurst was driven from Cleveland, Texas, to Natchez. Her escort (and alleged common-law husband), Edward Sebaugh,[200] drove Hurst to Nellie's house. The brunette Hurst was attractive, and so she was offered a room at Nellie's. She agreed to the price and promised to hand over half her earnings from future trysts. Because of the popularity of her new house, Hurst began making serious money. She most likely began to dream of setting enough aside to leave her current trade behind and begin a more tranquil and socially acceptable life.

The evening of June 2 began as most did evenings at Nellie's. Customers were invited into the kitchen. The girls came out and paraded before them. Then couples slipped into the back bedrooms. Not long after, the man would emerge and depart by the back door.

Only this night, no one came out. Nellie grew suspicious and knocked on the door, with no answer. When she entered, the window was open and her customer was gone. Only Estelle Hurst remained behind, lying on the bed with her throat slashed from ear to ear.[201]

Shortly after, police picked up twenty-four-year-old James Guy walking along a Natchez street with a bloody knife. He promptly confessed to killing

Hurst because she demanded five dollars after he had already prepaid her three dollars. Sebaugh was also arrested and admitted to transporting Estelle Hurst across state lines "for immoral purposes."[202]

There was now no doubt: Nellie Jackson was involved, at least indirectly, in trafficking in the human sex trade.[203] She was arrested, charged with running a "house of assignation," sentenced to six months in prison and fined $1,000. Nellie served her entire sentence.

Six months later, she was back running Nellie's, as busy as ever. Henceforward, Nellie would always carry a pistol with her and periodically knock on her girls' doors asking if everything was all right.[204]

1957–90

As successful as Nellie was becoming, she was careful not to upset the mores of the time. She presented herself as a humble but dignified Black woman. Police Chief Kenneth Fairly described Nellie as "very refined, distinguished looking….She dresses sedately, is well mannered and wears glasses."[205] She played the role of a boardinghouse mother (with the wink-wink skill of a successful entrepreneur), always careful not to cross certain lines. In a 1982 interview, Nellie reassured local citizens: "My place has a good reputation because it doesn't allow drugs inside."[206] Furthermore, she claimed to never recruit her girls. They simply showed up looking for work, and she gave them the means to support themselves.[207]

Nellie's most endearing (and/or business-savvy) quality was her generosity. Mayor Byrne explained: "She was very free with her money for charitable purposes. If someone was burned out she'd give them money, or if they were hungry. She never got credit for that. In the civil rights days, she bailed people out [of jail]. Even then nobody said anything about closing her up."[208] She was even known for giving rides to weary Catholic nuns.[209]

Nellie's generosity extended to the law as well. Each Christmas, she would deliver a fifth of Jack Daniel's whiskey to the mayor, along with a plea not to shut her down. Each mayor assured her that he had no intention of doing so. The sheriff would receive a homemade cake, while the police chief received bottles of liquor and the local nuns bottles of wine.[210]

Despite Nellie's generosity, a vocal minority of Natchez residents called for the prosecution of Nellie and the closure of her brothel. Those demands went unanswered. Nellie's had become an institution, and the woman behind it was all but untouchable. Even when she shot a peeping Tom in the butt (with the gun Nellie always carried after the Hurst murder), the charges were dismissed. Natchez police chief Kenneth Fairly explained, "Nellie Jackson is as much a part of Natchez as Main Street. I had just as soon try to shut down the Mississippi River bridge because people would not put up with it."[211]

NO MATTER HOW MUCH Nellie gave in bribes and charity, nothing would have saved Nellie from retaliation if her community had known of her other clandestine activity. They could turn a blind eye to her playing the role of a pimp or madam, but not an FBI informant. And certainly not an informant on matters of civil rights.

In 1964, the same year the bodies of Schwerner, Chaney and Goodman were unearthed in a Philadelphia, Mississippi dam, the FBI opened a field office in Natchez. Nellie Jackson entered its books as an informant. Now she had a new type of client—one she would meet at three or four o'clock in the morning, in her own private bedroom. The producer of the documentary *Mississippi Madam: The Life of Nellie Jackson*, Timothy Givens, explained: "FBI agents would go to her house at night. They would meet in the room where she did business. She was giving them information about the Klan. Her girls were gathering information from their dates. They would tell Nellie, and she would relay it to the FBI."[212]

Should Nellie's informant work ever become public knowledge, the consequences of a Black brothel owner working with the FBI in 1960s Mississippi need not be relayed. Attorney Bobby DeLaughter, who gained famed by finally placing Medgar Evers assassin Byron De La Beckwith in prison, noted that all civil rights workers were in danger of retaliation. A "snitch" or informant faced ten times the danger.[213]

Then again, Nellie had her infamous black book in which she recorded the names of her most famous and influential patrons. She had promised her customers absolute anonymity, and she went to her grave keeping her word. But her black book was insurance. Nellie Jackson had the power to stir up a whole lot of trouble in Natchez and beyond.[214]

Natchez
July 5–6, 1990

Nellie awoke on the morning of July 5, 1990. She slept in the front room by her screened-in porch. She could feel the early morning heat. The temperature would rise to ninety-two degrees by afternoon.[215] When she arose, she would have looked approvingly out her window at her neighbor's crab apples, which were beginning to bloom. She loved to bake crab apple pie. Some she ate, most she gave away—both on account of her natural (and calculated) generosity and her high blood pressure. The latter explained why she now cooked with so much garlic. Her beloved Dodgers were not helping with her blood pressure. They stood at 38-40, ten and a half games out of first place, having just lost their Fourth of July game to the Cubs.[216] On the flip side, business was still good. She had been a notorious and beloved celebrity for the past six decades, and the twilight of her life was a time of easy contentment. Nobody bothered her, and another lazy, humid Natchez summer entered its zenith.

Nellie went about her usual business that day, and her three girls went about theirs that evening. A little after midnight, there was a loud knock on the door. One of Nellie's girls, from Kalamazoo, Michigan, heard the pounding and the shouting. She saw a young man in shorts, shirt and tennis shoes. "He looked like a preppie. He had blond hair cut real short."[217] Daniel Eric Breazeale, an honor student at Ole Miss and prep school student from Madison, Mississippi, was looking for company. He was also drunk, and Nellie had a policy of not admitting drunks. Later, police lieutenant Ed Easton explained: "He was disgruntled because he could not be a customer. He was told to leave because he was too drunk."[218] Furious, Breazeale left the premises. He lived only a block away at 311 North Rankin Street but walked to a nearby gas station and bought an ice chest, which he filled up with gasoline.

Five hours later, Breazeale was back. This time, he brought a cooler of gasoline with him. He marched up the front steps. He then either entered the house or poured gasoline on Nellie through her screen door. In the process of toting the cooler or emptying it, he splashed some of the odorous fumes on himself. When Breazeale lit the fire, the porch and front room, Nellie, one of her dogs and Breazeale himself were engulfed in a fiery blaze.[219]

Six days later, Nellie would succumb to her burns. Nine days after Nellie, Breazeale passed away from the flames he ignited.

Natchez had lost one of its most notorious citizens—loathed by some, appreciated by more but mostly treasured for her celebrity.

Five years before Nellie's death, Ron Miller, the director of the Historic Natchez Foundation, explained the importance of Nellie Jackson to the Natchez community: "When people speak about Nellie's, they usually smile a little bit. I think there's a little fondness, not for Nellie's business, but for

Nellie Jackson's funeral service was held at St. Mary's Cathedral in Natchez. *Library of Congress.*

Nellie's. It adds a little spice to Natchez, a little odd quirk. Folks in Natchez are a little like those in England in that they value and cherish eccentricities, and Nellie's is an eccentricity."[220]

Thirty-three years after her death, a plan is in the works to memorialize Nellie Jackson and turn her house into a bed-and-breakfast with a museum honoring Natchez's most famous madam.[221]

Chapter 20

ANNE FRANÇOISE ROLAND

From "Prostitute" to Mother of the New World

St. Germain l'Aurerois Parish, France
1718

Anne's mother was dead. Her father remarried soon after—too soon for Anne. She despised her stepmother and began to rebel against her father. After all, she was a nineteen-year-old woman, coming of age and trying to find her own place in life. But then again, this was imperial France in 1719, and she was a nineteen-year-old woman. Frustrated with her rebellious ways, Anne's father notified the chief of police in Paris.[222]

February 13, 1719

Anne's father appeared before the king's counselor and testified against his daughter. He claimed that despite his constant and devoted care, Anne had gone astray. Her childish rebellions had grown to teenage rebellions, and now he feared that she had strayed too far from the path of righteousness. He had done all he could as a father, from the customary paternal care to enrolling her in a convent for two and a half years to apprenticing her at age seventeen to a dressmaker. Yet Anne remained incorrigible.

Anne's father learned that she was frequenting public dance halls, where she would meet young men and accompany them to wine houses. Eight days earlier, he had kept a vigilant eye on her all day, but then around 5:00 p.m., she disappeared after excusing herself to the bathroom. She was gone for the next five hours. A few days before that, "the day of Candlemas, his daughter having left the house at nine in the morning did not return to nine at night. When she knocked, the door was opened for her by the wife of the petitioner, her stepmother, who had been waiting for her, very worried considering the hour. The lady was amazed to find her with three men." Now he was turning his wayward daughter over to the law.[223]

Anne's father brought two of her uncles to testify against her, along with a letter from their parish priest stating, "I, undersigned priest, pastor of St. Germain l'Auxerrois certify that I have often heard complaints of the bad conduct of Anne-Françoise Rolland, my parishioner; that she has been reprimanded and advised in vain until now and that it would be [good] for her to be imprisoned."[224] Anne's father even offered to pay 100 livres per month for his daughter's upkeep should she be sent to the prison hospital for prostitutes.

The court record states:

> The said girl absented herself from the house [and] stayed out all night several times [and] this had happened very frequently last year without the plaintiff being able to find out nor discover where she was and whom she was with. Such a scandalous life has begun to dishonor the plaintiff and his family, and his said daughter, not being content with causing such a scandal and affront, she has, since the beginning of this year, redoubled her debaucheries in staying out all night more often and [she] earmarks the good feast days and chooses them for her debaucheries in spite of all the remonstrances—and punishment by the plaintiff.
>
> That which occasioned his being informed more exactly of her movements and learning that his said daughter frequented public dance halls along with flunkies.[225]

A woman who went out at night to enjoy herself, who attended parties unescorted and who stayed out past curfew was clearly up to no good. She was convicted of "debaucheries and public prostitution" and sentenced to the Salpêtrière Prison for prostitutes. The Marquis de Maurepas—for whom the first capital of Louisiana had been named—ordered Anne arrested on February 26. Three days later, he received the following message: "I have the honor of informing you that I have arrested and taken to [Salpêtrière] the said Anne-Françoise Rolland, following the King's order."[226]

A man pays a prostitute. *Bernard Picart, 1705, Rijksmuseum.*

Anne would not be imprisoned long. Just four months later, Dossier 12692 was filed: "This report contains the names of 209 persons imprisoned at the Salpetriere who are suitable to be sent to the islands, these women not being able to cause anything but public harm, being extraordinarily deprived of morals. In custody this 27 June 1719."[227] Anne's name was on page six.

Eight thousand miles away, the king's lands along the Mississippi Sound were floundering. John Law was trying to save the struggling colonies. But first, Governor Bienville needed wives for his colonists, and lots of them. Anne Françoise Roland became a pawn in the political game of empire building.[228]

View of the Hôpital de la Salpêtrière from the Seine. *Gabriel Perelle, 1677–95, Rijksmuseum.*

New France
1718

Bienville needed women—white women, as many as possible. His colony was floundering. Many of his men were off sleeping with Natives. Interracial relations did not bother Bienville. For an early eighteenth-century European, he had relatively progressive views when it came to the Native population.[229] He was concerned, however, about growing his colony into a metropolis along the lines of Quebec and a worthy satellite of Paris. To do so, he needed civilized men. More importantly, he needed civilized women who could tame his men. Instead, Paris sent him the dregs of French society.

Paris
1718–20

Unlike the English colonies to the east and the Spanish to the south, French Louisiana was struggling. Louis XIV's Gulf Coastal empire—now run by John Law—was depopulated. In answer, royal troops began scouring the streets of Paris for the unemployed and unwanted. They went to the prisons and offered deportation in lieu of extended prison sentences. And they went to the Salpêtrière Hospital—a prison for prostitutes—and found their women.

Many of the women in Salpêtrière were, in fact, prostitutes. However, a fair number happened to be in the wrong place at the wrong time, caught alone after dark or reported by disgruntled relatives as "immoral" women. Then again, the difference between a prostitute and an honest woman made little difference to a government that needed women for its colonies. All that mattered was they were young, healthy and possessed a womb.

New France
1719–22

Jesuit priest Father Pierre Charlevoix described the colonists being dumped into Bienville's capital at Biloxi:

> [The new arrivals] *are wretches, who being banished from France for their crimes or ill-behavior, true or supposed, or who, in order to shun the pursuits of their creditors, listed themselves among the troops, or hired themselves to the plantations…looking upon this country as a place of banishment only, were consequently shocked with everything: they have no tie to bind them nor any concern for the progress of a colony of which they are involuntary members.*[230]

In effect, as historian Ned Sublette claims, Louisiana was becoming the equivalent of twentieth-century Siberia: a penal colony. One batch of arrivals consisted of "160 prostitutes and 96 teenaged debauchees, from Paris's La Salpetriere house of correction for women; by 1721, this group had come to constitute 21 percent of the colony's female population."[231]

The odds of survival in early colonial Louisiana were dicey. The odds of flourishing were even worse. Most of the women forcibly sent to the young colony quickly married. A fair number soon abandoned their husbands and fled to larger "cities" and reverted to their old occupation. Venereal disease became rampant. (Eighty of these women released from Salpêtrière and condemned to Louisiana were first shackled in France to eighty recently released convicts and forcibly and publicly married before being sent aboard ship. No wonder so many of those marriages were unsuccessful in the New World!) The male immigrants also proved shiftless. Not accustomed to honest work in France, their habits followed them to Louisiana.[232]

It would take an incredible amount of savvy, perseverance and grit to survive in the world to which Anne Françoise had just been condemned.

1719–58

In December 1719, Anne set sail from Le Havre, France, on the ship *La Mutine*. The Salpêtrière women arrived on Dauphin Island on February 28, 1720, one year after Anne's arrest. Anne lived the life of the other women sent to Louisiana at Bienville's request and John Law's orders: the harrowing transatlantic ride; the arrival on a barren, white piece of sand that was supposed to resemble a city; the rats; the cholera; the lack of supplies; the lack of crops; the lack of housing; the lack of food; the uncertainty; the unfamiliarity; and the sense of dislocation.[233]

But Anne was stronger than her environment, tougher than the elements, and a natural survivor. She married the keeper of the colony's storehouse shortly after landing in the New World and soon gave birth to her first child.[234] A year after, she birthed a second son. At the time, her growing family lived on Chartres Street in the new capital of the Louisiana territory, New Orleans. Seven years later, Anne delivered a third son in Pointe Coupee (present-day Louisiana, roughly one hundred miles north of New Orleans). Two years later, Anne's husband died. She returned to New Orleans, and a year and a half later, she delivered another son, who was baptized shortly after. The father was recorded as "unknown." Three weeks later, the child was dead, and two weeks after the burial, Anne remarried an employee of the Company of the Indies.[235] Within three years, she added two more sons to her brood. Three years later, Anne again found herself widowed. Again she quickly found a husband, and this time, she bore him two daughters in quick succession, the last being born when Anne was in her early forties.[236]

In the 1745 census, Anne was again living in Pointe Coupee. Her elder three sons were no longer part of her household and were presumably living on their own, being in their late teens to mid-twenties. She was living with her four younger children and husband and had accumulated a modest fortune. Her family's possessions included two horses, eleven cattle, six slaves and twenty-three acres of cultivated land.[237]

Thirteen years later, in 1758, Anne Francois died in Pointe Coupee a modestly wealthy woman. Her most important legacy was the eight children she left behind. It was their descendants who would populate Mississippi, Louisiana, Arkansas and beyond.

Anne's final child was appropriately named Perine, or Petronille, the feminine of Peter, or "Rock." The uncontrollable young woman, "extraordinarily deprived of morals," discarded by her family and sentenced to prison and deportation ended up being the rock on which Mississippi and the Louisiana Territory were built.

Chapter 21

THE COTTON DISTRICT DANGLER

A Cool Sunday Morning in Starkville
Fall of 2017

The sun rose and Ben Stephens rose with it, although he did not want to. Stephens had been out late, playing pool and drinking beer at Dave's Dark Horse Tavern. Dave's was only a half mile from Stephens's apartment in the Cotton District, but Stephens had not wanted to make the walk home the night before; instead, he had slept at his friend's place near Dave's.

Stephens reckoned that it was shortly after five o'clock the next morning when he left his friend's house and began walking to his apartment on Lummus Street. He remembered the sky being a cloudless blue. And he remembered being "extremely, excruciatingly hungover." "I was trying to just orient myself in the world," he said. "I could barely see I was so hungover."

Stephens turned left onto University Drive and then right at Nash Street. Nash would take him to Lummus and the respite of his own bed.

Stephens remembered a black cat running across his path, into a yard of one of the small, close houses characteristic of the neighborhood. He watched the cat as it ran. "It ran off into the bushes," he said. "Then I looked up, and standing in the bushes was a man."

Stephens could not believe what he was seeing. The man in the bushes was wearing Vans shoes, a Herschel-style cap and nothing else. "I saw the

The view of a raised porch on Nash Street from an overgrown thicket. *Josh Foreman.*

dude—he was standing there either massaging himself or covering himself," Stephens said. "He had his hand on his penis."

The naked man looked at Stephens. Stephens looked at the naked man. Then Stephens started laughing. "That's a pretty bizarre sight, so it took me a second to process it. But once I had processed it, I started laughing like it was the funniest thing I had ever seen. I thought this was like a frat boy who had had his clothes stolen and was just trying to get home. I felt sorry for the guy."

As Stephens laughed, the man turned slowly and walked into some nearby trees. The whole encounter had lasted only a few seconds. Stephens would not understand until several months later that he had encountered a notorious Starkvillian. He was one of several people who had encountered the man in the early hours of the morning. He had come face to face with the man who had become known as the "Cotton District Dangler."[238]

THE COTTON DISTRICT IS Starkville's hippest neighborhood. Students want to live there, bars want to serve there and visitors want to stroll there. The brainchild of former Starkville mayor and developer Dan Camp, the neighborhood is a triumph of the New Urbanism movement. It is walkable and accessible, with houses, shopping, drinking and eating close together. Its small, two-story houses, narrow streets, porches, courtyards, fountains, shops and restaurants were inspired by iconic southern cities like New Orleans and Charleston and the Greek Revival and Victorian architectural styles.[239]

"New Urbanist streets are designed for people—rather than just cars," the Congress for the New Urbanism explains on its website. "We believe in providing plazas, squares, sidewalks, cafes, and porches to host daily interaction and public life."[240]

The Cotton District succeeds so well in its New Urbanist mission that, ironically, it made for the perfect roaming grounds of the Dangler. With its narrow streets, compact houses, foliage and—most importantly—frequent pedestrians, there were always people around, the constant chance for interaction, but not *too many* people. There would always be an alleyway to escape to or a house to hide behind or bushes to perch in.

By the time Ben Stephens ran into the Dangler in the fall of 2017, the Starkville Police Department had been getting reports of a "naked individual in the vicinity of University Drive" for at least six months. The pattern was the same—the Dangler was active between the hours of 5:00 a.m. and 6:00 a.m. and was always spotted in the Cotton District. Witnesses also reported that he came and went in a gray SUV.

Statuary characteristic of Starkville's Cotton District. *Josh Foreman.*

When Starkville PD began investigating sightings of the Dangler in February 2017, the sightings suddenly stopped. But six months later, with the arrival of fall, the sightings started up again. Starkville PD took the matter seriously and wanted to find the man roaming around with, as Chaucer may have put it, his "member of generation" dangling, his "nether purs" exposed to the chilly Starkville air.[241]

MISSISSIPPIANS HAVE KNOWN OF danglers before. In 1806, Natchez residents opened their newspapers to find the story of a dangler on the American frontier. The incident occurred in Danville, Kentucky, a town on the Wilderness Road visited by many people traveling to the frontier, including Meriwether Lewis and William Clark that same year.

A group of Shaker "fanatics" had passed through the town. One of them, a preacher, stripped off his clothes at the entrance to the town and walked the entire length of the main road carrying his hat, with his clothes laid over his arm and his private parts on display. As he walked, he shouted at the inhabitants of Danville, "Woe, woe, to the inhabitants of this place—for the judgment of God are hovering over them."

The inhabitants of Danville were appalled, and a group rode after the preacher. They captured him and brought him back to the town, where he was interrogated by a magistrate.

Why did you do it? The preacher explained himself by quoting a Bible verse, Isaiah 20:2–3: "At the same time spake the Lord by Isaiah the son of Amoz, saying, Go and loose the sackcloth from off thy loins, and put off thy shoe from thy foot. And he did so, walking naked and barefoot."[242]

But the preacher's explanation did not seem sincere. When the preacher left the town and reentered the wilderness, he put his clothes back on. His intent, clearly, had been to expose himself to the residents of the town. Without spectators, he preferred to be clothed.

The technical term for the behavior displayed by the preacher, and by the Cotton District Dangler more than two hundred years later, is exhibitionism. It is considered deviant, criminal sexual behavior. As psychotherapist Lisa Piemont wrote in a 2007 study, "It is a threatening act suggesting that the perpetrator intends a progression of his sexually aggressive behavior and indicating a dangerous incapacity to control impulses."

At the root of the behavior is a sense of boredom, emptiness or deadness in the exhibitionist. "The compulsion to sexually expose oneself appears to be commonly motivated by fears of psychic emptiness and interpersonal powerlessness," Piemont wrote. "The actions serve to provide stimulation, which prevents awareness of the psychic void." "They are ultimately most aroused by the shock and fear they elicit," Piemont continued.

And they are often disappointed—or even devastated—when their exhibition is met with an undesired response, such as laughter.[243]

IT WAS EARLY MORNING on Valentine's Day 2018. Two young men sat on their porch in the Cotton District, looking over at Nash Street. They were witnessing something curious: another man seemed to be hiding in the bushes, waiting for cars to pass by. When the cars passed, the man would emerge from the bushes and begin walking.

When the man stepped under a streetlight, the two witnesses realized that he was completely naked. And he was "playing with himself." The Dangler had been hiding from cars in the district, but when he looked up and saw that two men were watching him, he didn't hide at all. Instead, he stopped and, as a police report said, "began to stare at them."[244]

The Cotton District Dangler.
Josh Foreman.

A naked man walking down the street was a curious sight, but when the witnesses saw him touching himself—when he made eye contact with them—they felt disturbed. They left the porch and went inside, where they called Starkville police.

Starkville PD had been receiving reports of the Dangler for several weeks prior to Valentine's Day, and they had planned for when the next call came. Rather than approach the Cotton District in their squad cars, which had driven the Dangler underground before, they suited up in jogging clothes and hit the pavement on foot.[245]

The plan worked. They literally ran across the Dangler. He was put in handcuffs without incident and taken to the station downtown. His 2017 Ford Escape was towed.

The man they had arrested was twenty-two-year-old James Harmon Duke, a landscape architecture student at Mississippi State. Duke was originally from Hooks, Texas.

Starkville Police Department released a statement explaining that, after a year of searching, they had finally found the "naked individual" who had been repeatedly spotted in the Cotton District. Along with the statement, they posted Duke's mug shot. In it, a tall, thin man with a dark beard and wavy hair stares into the camera with expressionless eyes.[246]

Social media responses to the statement varied. Some people were frightened and glad of the arrest. "Good job SPD," one user wrote.

Others saw him as a mischievous free spirit. "Adam and Eve came to this world naked, and we are arresting people for it? Cool," another user wrote.

One user even advocated that he be "jailed and tortured so then they will remember to not do such things."[247]

Notably, users revealed the nickname that had been attached to the man over the course of the last year. "He has just been donned the District Dangler," a user wrote. "He's gonna be semi famous round campus." "They finally got the Cotton District Dangler," another user wrote. "Thank you!"

Duke was charged with seven misdemeanor counts of indecent exposure and bonded out. His case was ultimately "retired to the file." Under Mississippi law, prosecution of the case was suspended but could be reopened at any time at the discretion of the court.[248]

No sightings of the Dangler have been reported since.

NOTES

Pride

1. Jerry Mitchell, "Gunman Described as White Supremacist," *Clarion-Ledger*, April 14, 1996.
2. "2 Can Dine," advertisement, *Clarion-Ledger*, December 19, 1991.
3. Godfrey Jones and Belinda Moore, "How It Happened," infographic, *Clarion-Ledger*, April 14, 1996.
4. Will Pinkston and Josh Zimmer, "Sniper Terrorizes Shopping Area," *Clarion-Ledger*, April 13, 1996; Jones and Moore, "How It Happened"; "Lawmen Tracing Weapon Source of Jackson White Supremacist," *Clarksdale Press Register*, April 16, 1996; Jerry Mitchell, "'Turner Diaries' Transformed Disgruntled Vet, Ex-Wife Says," *Clarion-Ledger*, April 16, 1996.
5. Brad Franklin, "Forest Man Slain in Jackson Sniper Attack," *Scott County Times*, April 17, 1996; "Sniper's Victim's Family Recovering a Year Later," *McComb Enterprise-Journal*, April 14, 1997.
6. Steve Renfroe, "Law Officers Aid Citizens in 'Untold Stories of Heroism," letter to the editor, *Clarion-Ledger*, April 23, 1996; "Sgt. Renfroe Dedicates Life to Protecting Public," *Northside Sun*, June 14, 2001.
7. Josh Zimmer, "Authorities Not Certain How Sniper Obtained Array of Weapons," *Clarion-Ledger*, April 14, 1996.
8. Jay Hughes, "Injured Reporter Encourages People Not to Hate," *Clarion-Ledger*, April 14, 1996.
9. "Sniper Opens Fire on Blacks," *Orlando Sentinel*, April 14, 1996.
10. Jay Hughes and Butch John, "At Least 500 Rounds Sprayed by Sniper During Rampage," *Clarion-Ledger*, April 14, 1996.

11. Gregory Weber, "City Leader Cates Killed in Auto Fire," *Clarion-Ledger*, May 16, 1983.
12. Gregory Weber, "'The General' Lived Quietly in Small Town," *Clarion-Ledger*, June 10, 1983.
13. Kevin Havey et al., "More Pieces Found in Cates 'Jigsaw Puzzle,'" *Clarion-Ledger*, June 11, 1983.
14. "Mississippi Lawyer Believed Dead Held in Murder," *New York Times*, June 14, 1983.
15. Kevin Havey et al., "More Pieces Found."
16. Gougas Demmons and Kevin Haney, "Cates Back from 'Dead,'" *Clarion-Ledger*, June 10, 1983.
17. Ibid.
18. Robert Ourlian and Kevin Haney, "Friends Wonder Why Cates 'Caved InM'" *Clarion-Ledger*, June 10, 1983.
19. "Cates Tells Paper He Has 'Solid Defense,'" *Clarksdale Press Register*, July 26, 1983.
20. Beverly Pettigrew, "Work Begins Today on Identifying Body," *Clarion-Ledger*, June 18, 1983.
21. Greg Kuhl, "Ed Cates Sentenced to 20 Years," *Clarion-Ledger*, January 28, 1984.
22. Greg Kuhl, "A Year Later, Secrets Confined to Parchman with Cates," *Clarion-Ledger*, May 13, 1984.
23. Hairston, *Ole Miss 54*; Rhymes, *Ole Miss 57*.
24. Al Jernigan, e-mail message to Ryan Starrett, July 17, 2023.
25. Douglass, *Three Minute Man*, Kindle, location 274.
26. Ibid., location 185.
27. Ibid., location 143–85.
28. Ibid., location 1,703–76. Douglass's mistress referred to James as her "boyfriend" and her "Three Minute Man." Two witnesses told investigators that James paid his mistress for sexual favors.
29. Ibid., location 1,135.
30. Ibid., location 1,340–56.
31. While at the dealership, Mary Nell Jackson was on the phone with her friend Muriel Fisher. The phone call lasted until around 8:30 p.m. Therefore, the murder had to have occurred between the end of the call and James's 911 call at 8:56 p.m.
32. *Jackson v. State*, 551 So. 2d 132 (1989), https://law.justia.com/cases/mississippi/supreme-court/1989/57904-1.html.
33. Mark Rogers, "Book Details Infamous Killing," *Columbian-Progress*, September 29, 2018.
34. Douglass, *Three Minute Man*, location 3279.
35. E-mail correspondence with authors.
36. Douglass, *Three Minute Man*, location 3583.

Envy

37. Winders, *Panting for Glory*, 104, 165.

38. Robert Hindman, incidentally, also served in the Second Mississippi alongside his brother, Thomas, and William Falkner. Robert, however, remained a private throughout the conflict.

39. Find a Grave, "William C. Falkner," https://www.findagrave.com/memorial/5383/william-falkner.

40. "Death of Col. W.C. Falkner," *Clarion-Ledger*, November 14, 1889.

41. Haley Bracken, "Was There a Feud Between William Faulkner and Ernest Hemingway?," Britannica, https://www.britannica.com/story/was-there-a-feud-between-william-faulkner-and-ernest-hemingway.

42. Hotchner, *Papa Hemingway*, 75.

43. Faulkner, *As I Lay Dying*, 84.

44. Hemingway, *Green Hills of Africa*, 148–50. "That something I cannot yet define completely but the feeling comes when you write well and truly of something and know impersonally you have written in that way and those who are paid to read it and report on it do not like the subject so they say it is all a fake, yet you know its value absolutely; or when you do something which people do not consider a serious occupation and yet you know truly, that it is as important and has always been as important as all the things that are in fashion, and when, on the sea, you are alone with it and know that this Gulf Stream you are living with, knowing, learning about, and loving, has moved, as it moves, since before man, and that it has gone by the shoreline of that long, beautiful, unhappy island since before Columbus sighted it and that the things you find out about it, and those that have always lived in it are permanent and of value because that stream will flow, as it has flowed, after the Indians, after the Spaniards, after the British, after the Americans and after all the Cubans and all the systems of governments, the richness, the poverty, the martyrdom, the sacrifice and the venality and the cruelty are all gone as the high-piled scow of garbage, bright-colored, white-flecked, ill-smelling, now tilted on its side, spills off its load into the blue water, turning it a pale green to a depth of four or five fathoms as the load spreads across the surface, the sinkable part going down and the flotsam of palm fronds, corks, bottles, and used electric light globes, seasoned with an occasional condom or a deep floating corset, the torn leaves of a student's exercise book, a well-inflated dog, the occasional rat, the no-longer-distinguished cat; all this well shepherded by the boats of the garbage pickers who pluck their prizes with long poles, as interested, as intelligent, and as accurate as historians; they have the viewpoint; the stream, with no visible flow, takes five loads of this a day when things are going well in La Habana and in ten miles along the coast it is as clear and blue and unimpressed as it was ever before the tug hauled out the scow; and the palm fronds of our victories, the worn light bulbs of our discoveries and the empty condoms of our great loves float with no significance against one single, lasting thing—the stream."

45. Bracken, "Was There a Feud."
46. Kane, *Natchez on the Mississippi*, 460.
47. Ibid., 458.
48. Ibid.
49. Ibid., 466.
50. Grant, *Deepest South of All*, 226.
51. Ibid., 246.
52. Ibid., 245.
53. Kane, *Natchez on the Mississippi*, 468.
54. Ibid., 469.
55. Ibid., 470.
56. Grant, *Deepest South of All*, 34.
57. See Richard Ford's *Dispatches from Pluto: Lost and Found in the Mississippi Delta* (New York: Simon & Schuster, 2015).
58. Richard Grant quote, in Grant, *Deepest South of All*, 34.
59. Grant, *Deepest South of All*, 33.
60. Ibid., 34. The quotation is from Grant but captures the spirit of the Natchez Garden Club's views on their rivals.
61. Ibid., 246.
62. January Griffey, "Natchez Garden Club to Begin Its Own Pilgrimage," *Natchez Democrat*, January 7, 2023.
63. "River Pirates," *Natchez Weekly Courier*, January 40, 1840; "Eleven River Pirates Captured," *Daily Commercial Herald* (Vicksburg), December 14, 1889.
64. "The Houseboat Murder," *Vicksburg Herald*, July 23, 1901; "Last of Vogus Case," *Vicksburg Herald*, February 20, 1902; "Two Arrests in Houseboat Murder," *Commercial Appeal*, July 22, 1901.

Wrath

65. The ratio of Confederate dead to wounded was 1:7.5. Twice as many Confederates died of disease or as prisoners of war than were killed on the battlefield. A fascinating study by Ohio State University can be found at the following: https://ehistory.osu.edu/exhibitions/cwsurgeon/cwsurgeon/statistics. Although not citizens until the passage of the Fourteenth Amendment, seventeen thousand Black Mississippians also fought in the Civil War—nearly all on the side of the Union. Black soldiers, too, suffered significant casualties.
66. A friend of the Browns, John Johnson, was also involved in the shooting. In addition to charging Liddell with attempted murder, the Browns filed charges against six other men as well.
67. *The Conservative* (Carrollton, MS), February 20, 1886.
68. James, "Carrollton Courthouse 'Riot' of 1886."
69. *New York Times*, "An Epidemic of Lynching: The Result of Executive Clemency to Murderers," February 21, 1886.
70. *The Conservative* (Carrollton, MS), "Lynched," February 27, 1886.

71. James, "Carrollton Courthouse 'Riot' of 1886."
72. "The Carrollton Massacre," *Clarion-Ledger*, March 24, 1886; James, "Carrollton Courthouse 'Riot' of 1886"; Susie James, "They Didn't Want Us to Hate," *Clarion-Ledger*.
73. "Carrollton Massacre."
74. "Double Murder in McComb City," *Times-Picayune*, August 22, 1898.
75. The narrative here is drawn from witness testimony given during the second murder trial of Tom Garner. Garner was convicted of murder. "Garner Murder Trial," *Magnolia Gazette*, September 6, 1899.
76. "Garner Murder Trial."
77. "T.V. Garner Convicted," *McComb City Enterprise*, May 10, 1900.
78. "Causey Murder," *Times-Democrat*, September 5, 1899.
79. "Scott Causey and Wife Killed Near Summit," *Southern Herald*, August 26, 1898.
80. "Causey Murder."
81. "Wholesale Pardoning," *Natchez Democrat*, December 17, 1911.
82. Frank Jastrzembski, "The 'Black Knight'—Wild Fighter, Feared Duellist, and Hero of the Mexican—American War," War History Online, March 28, 2018, https://www.warhistoryonline.com/guest-bloggers/black-knights-heroism-mexican-american-war.html.
83. Jordan Rushing, "Famed Duelist of Vicksburg," *Vicksburg Daily News*, July 23, 2023.
84. Josh Edwards, "Gunfighter's Life Focus of Talk This Week; McClung Was Hero and Villain," *Vicksburg Post*, November 2, 2014.
85. Barbara Holland, "Bang! Bang! You're Dead: Dueling at the Drop of a Hat Was as European as Truffles, and as American as Mom's Apple Pie," *Smithsonian Magazine* (October 1997); Rushing, "Famed Duelist of Vicksburg."
86. *Cecil Whig* (Elkton, MD), April 7, 1855; Tommy Presson, "The Dueling Black Knight," *Vicksburg Daily News*, February 26, 2020. Information was also gleaned from the *Southern Marksman* (Clinton, MS), January 1, 1839. This story comes from the book *Invocation to Death: The Final Hours of Col. Alexander Keith McClung* by H. Grady Howell Jr. and is used with permission. The story also appears on the Mississippi Department of History and Archives website.
87. Ross Drake, "Duel! Defenders of Honor or Shoot-on-Sight Vigilantes? Even in 19th-Century America, It Was Hard to Tell," *Smithsonian Magazine* (March 2004).
88. Winders, *Panting for Glory*, 37, 51.
89. Jastrzembski, "Black Knight."
90. Edwards, "Gunfighter's Life Focus of Talk This Week."
91. Ibid.
92. Ibid.
93. Jastrzembski, "Black Knight."

94. Rushing, "Famed Duelist of Vicksburg."
95. Deavours, *Mississippi Poets*.

Sloth

96. Mitchell, *Mississippi*, 405–8.
97. Ibid., 447. Almost twenty-seven years later, De La Beckwith was finally convicted of the murder of Medgar Evers and sentenced to life in prison.
98. Ball, *Murder in Mississippi*, 73.
99. There are several theories as to how the FBI learned the location of the bodies. Some say that a mafia hit man, employed by the FBI, tortured the information out of a Klansman. Some say that a highway patrolman informed a friend at the FBI. Still others claim that the reward itself induced a caller to reveal the location.
100. Marsh, *God's Long Summer*, 144–45.
101. Ibid., 104–5.
102. Ibid., 142.
103. Father Bill Henry, "The Frozen Chosen," from a homily delivered at St. Francis of Assisi Catholic Church, Madison, Mississippi, on May 5, 2023.
104. Zola, "What Price Amos?: Perry Nussbaum's Career in Jackson, Mississippi," in Bauman and Kalin, *Quiet Voices*, 254.
105. Silver, *Mississippi*, 53.
106. Ball, *Murder in Mississippi*, 134–35.
107. Ibid., 80.
108. PBS News Hour, "Remembering Bill Minor, a Lion of Journalism in the South," March 28, 2017.
109. Marsh, *God's Long Summer*, 115.
110. Dittmer, *Local People*, 423.
111. Payne, *I've Got the Light of Freedom*, 349.
112. Silver, *Mississippi*, 142.
113. Ibid., 57.
114. Marsh, *God's Long Summer*, 45.
115. Isenberg, *White Trash*, 106–7.
116. Haynes, "Patrolling the Border," 9–10; Kokomoor, "Importance of the Oconee War," 30.
117. Lincecum, "Autobiography of Gideon Lincecum," 445–46.
118. Ibid., 447–48.
119. Spangler, "Becoming Baptists," 243–45.
120. Mulder, *Controversial Spirit*, 44–45.
121. In 2004, Kiah's great-great-great-great-grandson examined the church records from this time and discovered that there is no mention of the cat baptism. Instead, Kiah was excommunicated for racing on the Sabbath, refusing to head the church when called on and threatening to rape a woman. Lincecum, "Family Saga vs. History."
122. Lincecum, "Autobiography of Gideon Lincecum," 442–43.

123. Ibid., 443–70.
124. From numerous Father Joe Tonos homilies: the sin you can't remember is probably the one you're most guilty of.
125. In the same way Jimmy Buffett possessed a "license to chill." If there were such a degree, college campuses across the United States would no longer have recruiting issues.

Greed

126. Morris, *State Line Mob*, 181–83.
127. For future reference, the Shamrock Motel sat on the Tennessee side of the state line, while the restaurant and ballroom of the same name sat on the Mississippi side. The El Ray Motel is in Corinth, Mississippi, while the White Iris Club and Restaurant sat in McNairy County, Tennessee.
128. Both times, White lied about his age by three years.
129. Morris, *State Line Mob*, 49, 84.
130. Ibid., 111.
131. Ibid., 96–97.
132. Ibid., 140; "Armed Men Loot Casino on Coast," *Enterprise Journal*, March 25, 1965.
133. Morris, *State Line Mob*, 169.
134. Ibid., 170.
135. Purgatorio XXII, 42. White and Pusser were both carrying on an affair with the same Black woman.
136. Morris, *State Line Mob*, 126.
137. Ibid., 134.
138. Ibid., 148–50.
139. Ibid., 158–61. Pusser believed that Towhead White was behind his wife's assassination. However, no charges were ever filed, and the New Hope Road ambush remains a mystery. Regardless of White's involvement, no doubt the gangster was pleased to hear of the ambush.
140. There is some evidence that Towhead White had a large wad of cash in his pocket as well, but that money—if the rumors are true—never made it to the police station.
141. The murder of Towhead White remains a mystery. Rumors abound from a jilted lover to Buford Pusser himself. For the interested reader, W.R. Morris covers the murder of Towhead White in *State Line Mob*, 179–90.
142. DeRosier, "Natchez and the Formative Years."
143. DeRosier, *William Dunbar*, 27.
144. Ibid., 30–33.
145. Rowland, *Life, Letters, and Papers of William Dunbar*, 23.
146. DeRosier, "Natchez and the Formative Years."
147. Johnson, *Dictionary of the English Language*; Rowland, *Life, Letters, and Papers of William Dunbar*, 20–28.

148. Rowland, *Life, Letters, and Papers of William Dunbar*, 29–30.
149. DeRosier, *William Dunbar*, 34–35.
150. Ibid., 39–43.
151. The bet looks like a bad one to the authors, despite the odds being in Law's favor. (Was such a huge loss worth the minimal return?) But Law was likely trying to impress potential future patrons with his knowledge of all things monetary.
152. Boyle, "John Law."
153. Sublette, *World that Made New Orleans*, 48–49.
154. Boyle, "John Law."
155. Sublette, *World that Made New Orleans*, 50.
156. Myers, *1729*, 31.
157. Ibid., 143. The discerning and skeptical student of historiography will likely notice that the overwhelming majority of citations in the following section come from Kenneth Myers. While true, the authors highly recommend a perusal of Myers's work. It is a fascinating story written like a novel but based on all the primary sources available. Consequently, any attribution to Myers can be traced to an original source—a source he has so cleverly woven into his own narrative.
158. Ibid., 34.
159. Ibid., 35. The highest point of elevation in Louisiana is Driskill Mountain at 535 feet above sea level. Mississippi is much more mountainous on account of Woodall Mountain, which towers at 806 feet.
160. Ibid., 32–34.
161. Ibid., 31, 37.
162. Ibid., 62.
163. Powell, *Accidental City*, 53.
164. Ibid., 53.
165. Myers, *1729*, 31.
166. Ibid., 64.
167. Sublette, *World that Made New Orleans*, 52.
168. Ibid., 54. While the rumor's dissemination is fact, the story is almost certainly not.

Gluttony

169. Extreme Weather Watch, https://www.extremeweatherwatch.com/cities/jackson/year-1966.
170. Green, "Axe and You Shall Receive."
171. Tracy, *Mississippi Moonshine Politics*, 144.
172. Conforth and Wardlow, *Up Jumped the Devil*, 249–55.
173. Gene Trimble, "The Chip Board Archive 23," November 7, 2014, http://www.thechipboard.com/archives/archives.pl/bid/323/md/read/id/1320424/sbj/illegal-of-the-day-mississippi-8; *Clarion-Ledger*, "Two Killed in Rankin Gun Battle," August 28, 1946.
174. Tracy, *Mississippi Moonshine Politics*, 104–6.

175. Bivens did press charges but eventually recanted, and the two began associating again up and down the state line. Morris, *State Line Mob*, 117–21; "Restaurant Man Facing Charges," *Clarion-Ledger*, June 27, 1964.

176. Green, "Axe and You Shall Receive."

177. Chernow, *Grant*, 58.

178. Ibid., 58.

179. Ibid., 67.

180. Ibid., 69.

181. Foote, *Beleaguered City*, 107.

182. Ibid., 108.

183. Ibid., 107.

184. Ibid., 108.

185. Chernow, *Grant*, 272–77.

186. Ibid., 274–75.

187. Although Shelby Foote, Winston Groom, Charles Dana and Sylvanus Cadwallader offer their differing interpretations of Grant's Yazoo River "booze cruise" (and they are all worth reading), the following article sums up the divergent theories concisely and, in these authors' opinion, gets closest to the truth of Grant's June 5–6 Yazoo River adventure: "Truth Behind U.S. Grant's Yazoo River Bender: Murky Facts and Contradictions Confuse the Story of a Purported 1863 Drinking Spree by the General," Historynet, June 12, 2006, https://www.historynet.com/truth-behind-us-grants-yazoo-river-bender.

188. Craig Claiborne, "Just a Quiet Dinner for Two in Paris: 31 Dishes, 9 Wines, a $4,000 Check," *New York Times*, November 14, 1975.

189. Claiborne, "Just a Quiet Dinner for Two in Paris."

190. Jesse Yancy, "Elitist Eggs," *Mississippi Sideboard*, January 25, 2022, https://jesseyancy.com/tag/craig-claiborne.

191. The entirety of this vignette comes from two sources: Claiborne's own article in the *New York Times* on November 14, 1975, and the wonderful blog by Jesse Yancy, *Mississippi Sideboard*. (Simply search "Craig Claiborne" and you will find fascinating stories of the world-renowned, Mississippi-born food critic.)

Lust

192. Jerry Mitchell, "Fire Hurts Famed Natchez Brothel Owner," *Clarion-Ledger*, July 6, 1990.

193. Kelly, "Legend of Nellie Jackson."

194. Harvey Rice, "Natchez Sees Nellie's Place as Part of River City's Diversity," *Clarion-Ledger*, August 14, 1985.

195. *Mississippi Madam*.

196. Kelly, "Legend of Nellie Jackson."

197. Ibid.

198. Brian Broom, "Mississippi Madam," *Clarion-Ledger*, November 15, 2019.

199. Kelly, "Legend of Nellie Jackson."

200. Charles M. Hills, "Illegal House Operator Gets Stiff Sentence," *Clarion-Ledger*, June 22, 1957.

201. The documentary *Mississippi Madam* claims that Nellie chased Guy out of the house and proceeded to call the police.

202. "Wesson Man Admits Killing of Call Girl," *Clarion-Ledger*, June 4, 1957.

203. Although in the late 1960s several bordellos in the vicinity of Rankin Street were investigated for sex trafficking, Nellie Jackson was never charged. In her defense, she didn't seek out workers—they came to her. Kelly, "Legend of Nellie Jackson."

204. Kelly, "Legend of Nellie Jackson."

205. Rice, "Natchez Sees Nellie's Place."

206. Mitchell, "Fire Hurts Famed Natchez Brothel Owner."

207. *Mississippi Madam.*

208. Broom, "Mississippi Madam."

209. Ibid.

210. *Mississippi Madam.*

211. Mitchell, "Fire Hurts Famed Natchez Brothel Owner."

212. Broom, "Mississippi Madam."

213. *Mississippi Madam.*

214. The existence of the black book led one former Jackson lawyer to suggest that many in Natchez's power structure had an incentive to see Nellie protected. An attack on her or her business might lead to a retaliation many men in religious Natchez weren't prepared for.

215. Old Farmer's Almanac, "Weather History for Natchez, MS," https://www.almanac.com/weather/history/MS/Natchez/1990-07-05.

216. Baseball Reference, https://www.baseball-reference.com/boxes/?year=1990&month=07&day=4. Nellie was a huge baseball fan. Her home was decorated with pennants, and she attended several World Series, including the 1984 series at age eighty-two.

217. Leesha Cooper, "Natchez Brothel Owner Remains Critical," *Clarion-Ledger*, July 7, 1990.

218. Mitchell, "Fire Hurts Famed Natchez Brothel Owner."

219. Police Chief Ed Jones claimed that Breazeale poured gasoline on the porch, entered the house, poured the rest on Nellie and splashed himself in the process. "When he lit the fire at Nellie's, it blew him across the street." (Broom, "Mississippi Madam.") Nellie's sister, who lived on the same street, claimed that Nellie was "sitting on her bed with the screen door open. That's what she always did." (Cooper, "Natchez Brothel Owner Remains Critical.") The documentary Mississippi Madam claims that Nellie answered the door with a gun and that Breazeale splashed her through the slightly open door. One way or another, Breazeale splashed the gasoline on Nellie while she either stood or lay inside. In the hot summer, the main door was likely ajar, and the screen door was locked.

220. Rice, "Natchez Sees Nellie's Place."

221. Sabrina Simms Robertson, "Owner Seeks to Restore Nellie Jackson House," *Natchez Democrat*, July 14, 2021.

222. Sturgell, *My Louisiana Lineage*.

223. Ibid. Sturgell's entries on Anne Francois Roland include the original complaints of Anne's father, the rulings by the court and her arrest. She also has links next to each transcription to the original French papers. In short, Sturgell's research, organization and presentation are impressive.

224. Ibid.

225. "Notes for Anne Francoise Roland: Anne Francoise Rolland And Her Early Years In Paris," transcribed and submitted by Barbara Allemand Translated, edited and with a brief introduction by Winston DeVille, FASG (Bibliothéque de J. l'Arsenal, Archives de la Bastille, no. 10, 673), found at https://gw.geneanet.org/monartque?lang=en&n=roland&oc=0&p=anne+francoise.

226. Sturgell, *My Louisiana Lineage*.

227. "Notes for Anne Francoise Roland."

228. Mississippi was part of French Louisiana at the time of the story. Although the author generally uses the terms "Louisiana" or "Louisiana Territory," an important part of Anne's life was spent in what is now called Mississippi. (There is some evidence that she even spent some time in Natchez around the time of the infamous massacre.) The first and third of Louisiana's capitals were in present-day Mississippi: Ocean Springs and Biloxi. The second capital was in Mobile. After Biloxi was deemed impractical, New Orleans was made the center of Bienville's government.

229. Relatively.

230. Myers, *1729*, 31–32.

231. Sublette, *World that Made New Orleans*, 52.

232. Myers, *1729*, 33–34.

233. Ibid., 64–65.

234. The authors are not trained genealogists, and unfortunately, the genealogical record is often difficult to interpret and sometimes differs by website and researcher. A good amount of effort was put into making sure that this story is accurate in terms of Anne's children and the locales in which she lived. However, some of the dates and residences may be off. Yet such possible errors do not alter the main theme of Anne's incredible story of perseverance and survival.

235. Geni, "Anne Francois Roland," maintained by Joel Scott Cognevich, https://www.geni.com/people/Anne-Bordelon/6000000009716448994.

236. "Notes for Anne Francoise Roland."

237. Ibid.

238. "Ben Stephens" is a pseudonym. The man interviewed for this chapter asked that he not be identified. "Encounter with the Cotton District Dangler," Josh Foreman, interview by phone, December 7, 2023.

239. Congress for the New Urbanism, "Cotton District," https://www.cnu.org/what-we-do/build-great-places/cotton-district.

240. Ibid., "What Is New Urbanism?," https://www.cnu.org/resources/what-new-urbanism.

241. Geoffrey Chaucer, "The Wife of Bath's Prologue and Tale," Harvard's Geoffrey Chaucer website, https://chaucer.fas.harvard.edu/pages/wife-baths-prologue-and-tale-0.

242. "Not Common!," *Mississippi Herald and Natchez Gazette*, September 23, 1806.

243. Piemont, "Fear of the Empty Self."

244. Starkville Police Department, Offense/Incident Report, no. 18020131, Starkville, Mississippi, 2018.

245. Sarah Fowler, "MSU Student Accused of Walking Around Starkville Naked for a Year Charged," *Clarion-Ledger*, February 14, 2018.

246. Starkville Police Department, "Press Release. (Facebook)," February 14, 2018. https://www.facebook.com/starkvillepd/photos/a.543836412381907/149820 4243611781/?type=3.

247. Emmalyne Kwasny, "Student Arrested for Indecent Exposure," *Reflector*, February 14, 2018.

248. State of Mississippi, Starkville Municipal Court, Abstract of Court Record, Agency Code 5302, Citation no. MC1211171, Docket no. 1351065 (definition of "retired to file"), United States Court of Appeals for the Fifth Circuit, No. 06-61092, 2008.

SOURCES

Articles

DeRosier, Arthur H., Jr. "Natchez and the Formative Years of William Dunbar." *Journal of Mississippi History* 34, no. 1 (1972).

Haynes, Joshua "Patrolling the Border: Theft and Violence on the Creek-Georgia Frontier, 1770–1796." PhD diss., University of Georgia, 2013.

James, Susie. "Carrollton Courthouse 'Riot' of 1886." *Commonwealth* (March 12, 1996). http://www.vaiden.net/carrollton_massacre.html.

Kokomoor, Kevin. "The Importance of the Oconee War in the Early Republic." *Georgia Historical Quarterly* 105, no. 1 (2021).

Louisiana Historical Quarterly 3, no. 4 (October 1920).

Ohio State University. "Statistics on the Civil War and Medicine." https://ehistory.osu.edu/exhibitions/cwsurgeon/cwsurgeon/statistics.

Piemont, Lisa. "Fear of the Empty Self: The Motivations for Genital Exhibitionism." *Modern Psychoanalysis* 32, no. 1.

Rhymes, Fisher, ed. *The Ole Miss* 57 (1951). University of Mississippi.

Spangler, Jewel L. "Becoming Baptists: Conversion in Colonial and Early National Virginia." *Journal of Southern History* 67, no. 2 (2001).

Sturgell, Cathy Lemoine. My Louisiana Lineage. http://louisianalineage.com/b5773.htm.

Ward, Rick. "The Carroll County Courthouse Massacre, 1886: A Cold Case File." Mississippi History Now, May 2012. https://www.mshistorynow.mdah.ms.gov/issue/the-carroll-county-courthouse-massacre-1886-a-cold-case-file.

Books

Ball, Howard. *Murder in Mississippi:* United States v. Price *and the Struggle for Civil Rights.* Lawrence: University Press of Kansas, 2004.

Bauman, Mark K., and Berkley Kalin. *The Quiet Voices: Southern Rabbis and Black Civil Rights, 1880s to 1990s.* Tuscaloosa: University of Alabama Press, 1997.

Chernow, Ron. *Grant.* New York: Penguin Press, 2017.

Conforth, Bruce, and Gayle Dean Wardlow. *Up Jumped the Devil: The Real Life of Robert Johnson.* Chicago: Chicago Review Press Incorporated, 2019.

Deavours, Ernestine Clayton. *The Mississippi Poets.* Memphis, TN: E.H. Clarke & Brother, 1934.

DeRosier, Arthur H., Jr. *William Dunbar, Scientific Pioneer of the Old Southwest.* Lexington: University Press of Kentucky, 2007.

Dittmer, John. *Local People: The Struggle for Civil Rights in Mississippi.* Champaign: University of Illinois Press, 1995.

Douglass, Richard L. *The Three Minute Man: The Story of a Small Town Sociopath.* New York: Page Publishing, 2018.

Faulkner, William. *As I Lay Dying.* New York: Vintage International, 1985.

Foote, Shelby. *The Beleaguered City: The Vicksburg Campaign.* New York: Modern Library, 1995.

Grant, Richard. *The Deepest South of All: True Stories from Natchez, Mississippi.* New York: Simon & Schuster, 2021.

Groom, Winston. *Vicksburg, 1863.* New York: Vintage Books, 2010.

Hemingway, Ernest. *Green Hills of Africa.* New York: Scribner, 1963.

Hotchner, A.E. *Papa Hemingway.* New York: Bantam Books, 1967.

Isenberg, Nancy. *White Trash.* New York: Viking, 2016.

Johnson, Samuel. *Dictionary of the English Language.* Dublin: W.G. Jones, 1768.

Kane, Harnett Thomas. *Natchez on the Mississippi.* Potomac, MD: Pickle Partners Publishing, 2016.

Lincecum, Gideon. "Autobiography of Gideon Lincecum." *Publications of the Mississippi Historical Society* 8 (1904).

Lincecum, Jerry Bryan. "Family Saga vs. History: Hezekiah Lincecum and the Church." In *Both Sides of the Border.* Denton: University of North Texas Press, 2004.

Marsh, Charles. *God's Long Summer: Stories of Faith and Civil Rights.* Princeton, NJ: Princeton University Press, 1997.

Mitchell, Dennis J. *Mississippi: A New History.* Jackson: University Press of Mississippi, 2014.

Morris, W.R. *The State Line Mob: A True Story of Murder and Intrigue.* Nashville, TN: Rutledge Hill Press, 1990.

Mulder, Philip N. *A Controversial Spirit: Evangelical Awakenings in the South.* Oxford, NY: Oxford University Press, 2002.

Myers, Kenneth M. *1729: The True Story of Pierre & Marie Mayeux, the Natchez Massacre and the Settlement of French Louisiana.* Denison, TX: Mayeux Press, 2017.

Payne, Charles M. *I've Got the Light of Freedom: The Organizing Tradition and the Mississippi Freedom Struggle*. Berkeley: University of California Press, 1995.

Powell, Lawrence N. *The Accidental City: Improvising New Orleans*. Cambridge, MA: Harvard University Press, 2012.

Rowland, Dunbar. *Life, Letters, and Papers of William Dunbar*. Jackson: Mississippi Historical Society, 1930.

Silver, James W. *Mississippi: The Closed Society*. New York: Harcourt, Brace & World, 1964.

Sublette, Ned. *The World that Made New Orleans: From Spanish Silver to Congo Square*. Chicago, IL: Lawrence Hill Books, 2009.

Tracy, Janice Branch. *Mississippi Moonshine Politics: How Bootleggers & the Law Kept a Dry State Soaked*. Charleston, SC: The History Press, 2015.

Winders, Richard Bruce. *Panting for Glory: The Mississippi Rifles in the Mexican War*. College Station: Texas A&M University Press, 2016.

Court Records

State of Mississippi, Starkville Municipal Court.

Documentaries

Mississippi Madam: The Life of Nellie Jackson. Directed by Timothy Givens and Mark Brockway. 2017.

Websites

almanac.com.
baseball-reference.com.
britannica.com.
chaucer.fas.harvard.edu.
cnu.org.
columbianprogress.com.
ehistory.osu.edu.
extremeweatherwatch.com.
facebook.com.
findagrave.com.
geneanet.org.
geni.com.
historynet.com.
jesseyancy.com.
law.justia.com.
lawlit.net.
louisianalineage.com.

pbs.org/newshour.
smithsonianmag.com.
thechipboard.com.
warhistoryonline.com.

Newspapers

Cecil Whig (Elkton, MD).
Clarion-Ledger (Jackson, MS).
Clarksdale (MS) Press Register.
Columbian-Progress (Marion County, MS).
Commonwealth (Greenwood, MS).
Conservative (Carrollton, MS).
Daily Commercial Herald (Vicksburg, MS).
Magnolia (MS) Gazette.
McComb (MS) City Enterprise.
Mississippi Herald and Natchez Gazette.
Natchez Democrat.
Natchez Weekly Courier.
New York Times.
Northside Sun (Jackson, MS).
Orlando (FL) Sentinel.
Reflector (Starkville, MS).
Scott County Times (Forest, MS).
Southern Herald (Liberty, MS).
Times-Democrat.
Times-Picayune (New Orleans, LA).
Vicksburg (MS) Daily News.
Vicksburg (MS) Post.

Podcasts and Lectures

Boyle, Patrick. "John Law—The First Financial Engineer—A History of Paper Money and the Mississippi Bubble." YouTube. Uploaded by Patrick Boyle on Finance. https://www.youtube.com/watch?v=H5uKPUPQSyQ.

Green, Josh. "Axe and You Shall Receive: The 1966 Jackson Mississippi Country Club Liquor Raid." MDAH History Is Lunch talk, August 19, 2020. YouTube. https://www.youtube.com/watch?v=AHa99CF5JPM.

Kelly, Erica (host). "The Legend of Nellie Jackson." *Southern Fried True Crime*, episode 145. YouTube. https://www.youtube.com/watch?v=DEy4MPfVJE8.

ABOUT THE AUTHORS

RYAN STARRETT was birthed and reared in Jackson, Mississippi. After receiving degrees from the University of Dallas, Adams State University and Spring Hill College, he has returned home to Mississippi to continue his teaching career. He lives in Madison, Mississippi, with his wife, Jackie, and two children, Joseph Padraic and Penelope Rose O. *Wicked Mississippi* is one among a number of southern-themed books he has written with his oldest friend, Josh Foreman. Their other projects can be perused at foremanstarrett.com.

JOSH FOREMAN IS FROM Jackson, Mississippi. His second home is Seoul, South Korea, where he lived, taught and traveled from 2005 to 2014. He holds degrees from Mississippi State University and the University of New Hampshire. He lives in Starkville, Mississippi, with his wife, Melissa, and his three children, Keeland, Genevieve and Ulrich. He teaches journalism at Mississippi State University.

Visit us at
www.historypress.com